Values and Ethics in Mental Health Practice

Other books in this series

Books in the Mental Health in Practice series

To order, please contact our distributor: BEBC Distribution, Albion Close, Parkstone, Poole, BH12 3LL. Telephone: 0845 230 9000, email: **learningmatters@bebc.co.uk**.

You can also order online at **www.learningmatters.co.uk**.

Values and Ethics in Mental Health Practice

DAISY BOGG

Series Editor: Keith Brown

First published in 2010 by Learning Matters Ltd

British Library Cataloguing in Publication Data
A CIP record for this book is available from the British Library.

ISBN: 978 1 84445 375 7

This book is also available in the following formats:

Adobe ebook ISBN: 978 1 84445 775 5
EPUB ebook ISBN: 978 1 84445 774 8
Kindle ISBN: 978 0 85725 028 5

Cover and text design by Code 5 Design Associates Ltd
Project management by Swales & Willis Ltd, Exeter, Devon
Typeset by Swales & Willis Ltd, Exeter, Devon
Printed and bound in Great Britain by TJ International Ltd, Padstow, Cornwall

Learning Matters Ltd
33 Southernhay East
Exeter EX1 1NX
Tel: 01392 215560
info@learningmatters.co.uk
www.learningmatters.co.uk

FSC
Mixed Sources
Product group from well-managed
forests and other controlled sources
Cert no. SGS-COC-2482
www.fsc.org
© 1996 Forest Stewardship Council

Contents

Foreword to the Post-Qualifying Social Work Practice series

All the texts in the Post-Qualifying Social Work Practice series have been written by people with a passion for excellence in social work practice. They are primarily written for social workers who are undertaking post-qualifying social work awards, but will also be useful to any social worker who wants to consider up-to-date practice issues.

The books in this series are also of value to social work students as they are written to inform, inspire and develop social work practice.

Professor Keith Brown
Series Editor
Centre for Post-Qualifying Social Work, Bournemouth

About the author

A social worker by background, Daisy has spent a large part of her career working in integrated health and social care environments, looking at how to develop and implement more seamless service provision across the two agendas. She most recently held the role of Executive Director of Social Care and Specialist Services for Bedfordshire and Luton Partnership NHS Trust, which she left in March 2010 to become an independent consultant specialising in social approaches to mental health, providing training, development and interim management services within mental health services. Daisy is an executive committee member of the Social Perspectives Network (SPN), a national organisation made up of professionals, academics and service users who specialise in promoting the social perspective within mental health policy and provision across the UK. She has worked within mental health and addiction services for the last fifteen years, both for the NHS and also for voluntary sector organisations.

Acknowledgements

As always, a big thank you is due to my husband, Terry, for being my human thesaurus and live-in grammar checker.

Thanks also to Lauren and Luke for their support and comments throughout this project. Writing something like this can be an isolating process, and being able to get feedback at each stage helps to keep things going in the right direction (and convinces me I'm not just making things up). Thanks also to Keith Brown and Rob Goeman for their comments and feedback, and to Alleyn for sharing her experiences.

There are a few people out there who remind me why Approved Mental Health Professional (AMHP) practice is so important, and so to Wendy and Claire (and this year's cohort of students who sat through my dual diagnosis rants), thanks are also due to all of you.

Introduction

This book considers the development of the value base associated with mental health practice and considers both approved mental health practice and best interest assessment. By considering the range of social, policy and legislative frameworks, as well as the evidence base for mental health treatment, and applying these to ethical and value-based practice, this book aims to discuss some of the dilemmas faced by professionals in the practice environment.

A number of areas are covered, the aim being to provide a detailed context in which practice occurs and provide a theoretical foundation for practitioners to understand and develop their skills and knowledge.

The areas considered include:

- Professional values and ethics.

- Historical perspectives on mental health law and practice.

- The role of social values in shaping value-based practice.

- Human rights issues and practice within this framework.

- Complex and multiple needs and identities.

- Ethical dilemmas facing practitioners.

- Power relationships and the impact of decision making on both service users and practitioners.

- The impact of the guiding principles and code of practice in statutory roles.

The study of values and ethics is not an exact science, and there are a range of influences that shape decisions and interventions; as such, the aim here is not to provide concrete solutions but rather to highlight some of the dilemmas and debates evident in current practice and encourage practitioner reflection.

The book is in three parts. Chapters 1–4 provide the background and context in which mental health services are developed and delivered. Chapters 5–7 concentrate on particular human rights and how these are applied within practice, and Chapters 8 and 9 look at particular issues that practitioners may face in the course of their work. All three parts encourage professional reflection as a core part of value-based practice, and the final chapter attempts to draw together all of the discussions to promote an overall approach based on values and ethics in practice.

Chapter 1 The development of the social work and mental health value bases

This chapter considers the development of value-based practice both within social work and in wider mental health practice.

Chapter 2 Ethics, social values and mental health treatment

Social values are considered in more detail in this chapter. Issues such as societal responses to mental health, and how these shaped the development of the value base and practice framework, are the main focus of the discussion.

Chapter 3 The development of mental health law

This chapter continues the discussion about social values and considers the context of the legislation within which mental health operates. This includes both a historical view of how mental health law has developed in the UK and the role of values/principles and Codes of Practice.

Chapter 4 Values in approved practice: empowerment and enforcement

The AMHP role is a balancing act owing to the duality of its nature – protection of individual and protection of public – and this chapter considers some of the associated ethical issues.

Chapter 5 Equality and diversity

The six strands of equality (gender, age, race, religion, sexuality and disability) are the central foci of this chapter, with discussions based on the development of cultural competence and equality-based practice. This chapter is co-authored by Daisy Bogg and Harjinder Bahra. Harjinder is an equality and human rights barrister specialising in health and social care. He has advised on equality, diversity, multiculturalism, community cohesion and human rights in various capacities over the last decade. His passion for dignity and respect for all has made him one of the leading campaigners on embedding human rights outcomes in service access and delivery. He is a contributor to the Department of Health's *Human Rights in Healthcare – A Framework for Local Action*. In addition to working as an independent consultant, Harjinder is currently the interim equality and diversity manager at South Essex Partnership Mental Health Foundation Trust (SEPT) and also NHS Southwark.

Chapter 6 Rights and self-determination

The principles of best interests and self-determination are explored in this chapter. Participation and involvement are key aspects of mental health practice, and part of the Codes of Practice for both mental health and mental capacity law.

Chapter 7 Privacy and dignity

Privacy and dignity are key elements of practice in modern mental health services. This includes a range of considerations such as environment, communication and treatment options, and practitioners need to demonstrate awareness and ability to advocate for an individual's rights.

Chapter 8 Effective safeguarding

Safeguarding is an area in which all professionals have a duty, and this chapter considers the issues associated with safeguarding that may be encountered by AMHPs, Best Interests Assessors (BIAs) or social workers in mental health care.

Chapter 9 Capacity

An individual's capacity to make a decision is a core consideration in mental health practice, and practitioners need to be aware of this and equipped to make assessments and decisions regarding an individual's ability in this area. This chapter considers capacity and consent issues in mental health care.

Chapter 10 Complex needs

This chapter considers some of the complexities that are evident in practice for individuals who have traditionally been viewed as more complex service users. Dual diagnosis and personality disorders, including the service responses to these issues, are considered. This includes the impact of prejudices on practice, applying the exclusions under the Act, and appropriate treatment/service availability.

Conclusion

This section brings together the varying frameworks and issues presented to summarise the range of value-based decision making and ethical considerations that are evident within mental health as a whole, and AMHP and BIA roles in particular.

At the time of writing this book the NHS white paper *Equity and Excellence: Liberating the NHS* had just been published for consultation. The intentions of the coalition government for the future of health services include localising the commissioning of services into GP consortiums that will be responsible for ensuring that local health needs are met. Whilst local authorities will still have responsibility for statutory mental health, including the AMHP roles, the shift towards GP consortiums as the major health commissioners, and the abolition of primary care trusts (PCTs), will have a significant impact on how mental health services are delivered in the future, and is an area that mental health practitioners will need to remain aware of as the final proposals are published and implemented.

Chapter 1

The development of the social work and mental health value bases

CHAPTER OBJECTIVES

This chapter will assist readers in meeting the following mental health national occupational standards as relevant to all professional groups, including the statutory roles of AMHP and BIA under mental health and mental capacity legislation.

- A3 Promote the values and principles underpinning best practice.
- B2 Enable people with mental health needs to access and use services effectively and in ways that promote their rights.
- O9 Promote people's equality and respect for diversity.

The hope of a free man in a frightened world is the values which man puts ahead of inventions when his back is to the wall.

Ralph W. Sockman (1889–1970), American Methodist pastor

Introduction

Professional values are an integral part of modern mental health practice regardless of professional discipline, and the principles of respect, participation and self-determination now cross the professional divides. For social workers in mental health settings this is familiar ground, and the discipline has traditionally worked with a value base that supports partnership and the rights of individuals.

Values and ethics are both difficult to define, as they are a collection of beliefs and attitudes that are generally shaped by both experience and environment. Social work values have developed alongside psychiatric ethics, and the increasing participation of users in service delivery has contributed to a more person-centred approach based on the principles of human rights, social welfare and social justice. The voice of the service user movement has been significantly strengthened over the past 50 years, and the disability movement, which defines the recovery approach as one of individual experience and empowerment, has ensured that professional values and approaches have become focused on the needs, wishes and aspirations of the individual user and their support networks.

Although mental health services are becoming increasingly multidisciplinary, and traditional social care roles, such as the approved mental health professional (AMHP), are now extended across several professions, the core social work values and the principles of the social model of disability are pervasive within both policy and practice. It is therefore useful for practitioners to understand how these have developed, and to have an awareness of the evidence base on which they rest.

As service delivery has shifted towards user choice, control and empowerment, so too has the debate around values shifted from professional values to the personal values of those who use services (Woodbridge and Fulford, 2003; Beigel and Santiago, 1995; Banks, 2006), and this has required professional adjustment and changes in the power dynamic between worker and service user. The expansion of the recovery approach across service delivery, which espouses self-efficacy and self-determination as its key principles (Anthony, 1993; Deegan, 1996; SCIE/RCP, 2007), has further contributed to this shift. The policy of personalised services, controlled by the individual, means that the emphasis on the person's values and expectations should be a primary concern for professional practice.

The relationship between ethics and values

Values are a complex phenomenon and are difficult to define with clarity: they take into account the beliefs and attitudes of the individual and are influenced by their social context and experiences (Woodbridge and Fulford, 2003; Chief Nursing Officer, 2006; Barnard, 2008).

Professional values have for many years been a focus of training and continuing professional development, as a result of the recognition that an individual's value base influences their decisions and actions. When working with vulnerable groups, who may be unable to articulate their own wishes or are otherwise experiencing powerlessness, it is essential that the practitioner does not allow their own preconceived ideas or prejudices to negatively affect their response to, or the welfare of, those they are working with.

In the area of professional ethics the term 'values' is generally used to describe general ethical principles relating to how professionals treat the people they work with; however, in social work this is further developed to include beliefs, assumptions and norms, and how these affect practice situations (Woodbridge and Fulford, 2003; Banks, 2006; Barnard 2008; Gilbert, 2003; Payne, 2006).

REFLECTION POINT

- *What are the personal values that you bring to your practice?*
- *Where do these values come from and what influences them?*
- *Is there a difference between your personal and professional values?*
- *How do these inform your decisions?*

Comment

Personal values such as a commitment to social justice or a belief in equality are translated into the practice situation. Social work is centred on the relationship between the individual and their social system, and the same principles apply to the practitioner and the need to be a source of reflection. Practitioner reaction to service user behaviours and circumstances is guided by personal and professional values and interpretation, and to maintain competence a critical review of practice is needed.

The development of the social work value base

The development of social work as a profession is heavily influenced by the sociopolitical context of the home nation, and hence the roles and practices of the profession therefore vary between countries. Despite these influences the value base of social workers appears to be consistent in the international context, and it is interesting to note that although roles may be different, the definitions of the values that shape the profession are common.

The first mental health social workers appeared in England during the 1920s as visitors to individuals in the large psychiatric asylums. Before this time the social welfare practices that had been developing were more informal activities based on the social welfare reformist movement, and operated by charity and faith organisations (Payne, 2006; Gilbert, 2003; Bogg, 2008; DoH, 2007a). These foundations mean that in the early years, when the professional began to take on a more formal role, social work was based on social welfare ideals.

Social work has changed over time and represents the social values of its time; as such, it has been suggested that there have been distinct periods within the historical development of the social work value base. Reamer (2006) argues that there are four stages that can be observed as social work moved from being a charitable activity to a professional one, whereas Rojeck et al. (1988) defined social work values as ideas received from society about professional values and standards of practice in relation to 'the technical management of personal problems and the maintenance of order' (p.1). In this understanding the social progress and advances in the effectiveness of treatment result in a shift of the value base from morality and social conscience to empowerment and rights, and into what is now an evidence- and value-based approach.

RESEARCH SUMMARY

Reamer's model of the development of the social work value base

Reamer's work (2006) charted the development of the social work value base and identified four distinct historical periods.

- **Morality period** *(late nineteenth century)*
  Concentrated on the morality of the service user; took a paternalistic approach to providing for the poor and 'wayward', and addressed the morality of those in need.

- **Values period** *(early twentieth century)*
  Social work shifted from concern for morality towards the need for dramatic social reform in the areas of housing, health, sanitation, employment, poverty and education.

- *Ethical theory and decision-making period* (1940s and 1950s)
  Morality again became a focus, but this time centred on the morality and ethics of the profession and its practitioners. Ethical guidelines were developed and professional conduct considered.

- *Ethical standards and risk management period* (1960 onwards)
  Attention shifted to the ethical constructs of social justice, rights and reform. This reflected the political mood and was consistent with the civil rights developments of the time, and has continued to develop into what are now the codes of practice and occupational standards that govern social work as a profession.

This model demonstrates how the values of social work have changed, and these values are reflected in the social context of the times (see Chapter 2 for an in-depth discussion). Social work is considered to be a value based profession (IFSW, 2004; BASW, 2002), and as a result what is considered good practice is dependent upon the social context in which it operates.

Contemporary social work

The development of the civil rights movements and the increasing voice of the mental health survivor groups during the last century have helped make some progress towards implementing the social model in mental health. This is particularly evident within the policy and practice frameworks that have been developed, and is supported by the increased emphasis on service user experience and recovery across mental health environments (Duggan et al., 2002; Ray et al., 2008).

It can be argued that whereas medical approaches may remain valid and have a contribution to make, the social model has been embraced by both social care practitioners and service users and informs a large proportion of the policy that now guides the delivery of services (Ray et al., 2008; Shaping Our Lives et al., 2007; DoH, 1999a, 2009a). It should be noted that the delivery of mental health services may not fully reflect the policy shift towards social understanding, and in many services there remains a medically dominated approach that does not necessarily allow for an improved or holistic experience for those who use services.

Social work as a profession has undergone significant scrutiny and change over the last decade, with professional registration and a new Code of Practice being enshrined in legislation, and a number of surveys and debates have been carried out in an attempt to identify, clarify and explore the role of social work and its value in society (CSIP/NIMHE, 2006; Parrott, 2006; Merchant, 2007; Ray et al., 2008; Scottish Executive, 2006; DoH, 2007a).

Following a number of high-profile debates and incidents, in 2009 the Social Work Task Force was established as a joint initiative between the Department of Health and the Department of Children, Schools and Families (Social Work Task Force 2009a; 2009b). Its aim was to undertake a comprehensive review of social work practice and to make recommendations for improvement and reform of the whole profession. The membership was broad and included practitioners, managers, researchers, third-sector representatives and service user organisations. In its interim report, which was published in July 2009, the value of the social work profession was defined as:

> *Social work helps adults and children to be safe so they can cope and take control of their lives again. Social workers make life better for people in crisis who are struggling to cope, feel alone and cannot sort out their problems unaided.*

(Social Work Task Force, 2009a; p.10)

Consideration of a value based profession is implicit in these definitions as they concentrate on empowering service users and providing support. The task force concluded that the role of social work is valued by users as it approaches individuals in a non-judgemental manner and promotes equality and self-determination; however, it needs to be strengthened and supported to provide practitioners with the opportunity to develop critical practice and intervene appropriately in situations where adults, children and the community are at risk. The taskforce made 15 recommendations that would assist in this aim and which would create a clear professional structure:

- The criteria for entry to social work education and training should be strengthened to ensure high-quality candidates.

- An overhaul of the content and delivery of social work degree courses to make them fit for purpose and prepare practitioners for practice environments.

- Provide sufficient high-quality practice placements, which are properly supervised and assessed.

- The introduction of an assessed and supported year in employment as the final stage in becoming a social worker.

- More transparent and effective regulation of social work education to give greater assurance of consistency and quality.

- The development of a clear national standard for the support social workers should expect from their employers in order to do their jobs effectively.

- The new standard for employers should be supported by clear national requirements for the supervision of social workers.

- The creation of dedicated programmes of training and support for front-line social work managers.

- The creation of a more coherent and effective national framework for the continuing professional development of social workers.

- The creation of a single, nationally recognised career structure which allows practitioners to stay in practice in advanced roles.

- The creation of an independent national college of social work developed and led by social workers.

- A new programme of action on public understanding of social work.

- The development of a 'licence to practise' system for social workers.

- A new system for forecasting levels of supply and demand for social workers.

- The creation of a single national reform programme for social work.

(Social Work Task Force, 2009b)

The social work task force has been accepted by government and at the time of writing the recommendations are being further scoped for implementation. This study and report represents a clear statement from authorities about the commitment to and value of social work in society, and is a recognition that the roles that social work undertakes are often with the most risky and deprived groups. It is also recognition of the values that guide the profession, as it identifies that social work needs to be supported if it is to respond and practise ethically and appropriately with individuals and groups who may be on the margins of society.

Professional values across disciplines

Social work is not the only profession to develop a set of basic values. Psychiatric ethics and values in nursing practice have also continued to develop, and allied health professionals (AHPs) such as occupational therapists (OT) and psychology practitioners would also argue that they have a distinct value base (Chief Nursing Officer, 2006; Bloch and Green, 2009; COT, 2005, 2008; BPS, 2009). These values are all very similar and emphasise the individual's needs: for example, the Royal College of Nursing state that the nursing profession's values include being *inclusive, listening, caring and respectful* in all aspects of the work (RCN, 2003), and the British Association of Occupational Therapy include an emphasis on individual autonomy and welfare (COT, 2005).

The move towards multidisciplinary approaches and services that have a more recovery-orientated ethos has led to the development of shared values across professional groups in recent years, and these reflect the person-centred nature of mental health policy, with anti-discrimination, empowerment and self-determination being key factors.

Following the publication of the National Service Framework (DoH, 1998), which emphasised the need for a multidisciplinary approach to service delivery, a number of best-practice guides were published. These included the Sainsbury Centre's framework *The Capable Practitioner* (SCMH, 2001), the Department of Health's document *The Ten Essential Shared Capabilities: A Framework for the Whole of the Mental Health Workforce* (Hope, 2004), and *Capabilities for Inclusive Practice* (DoH, 2007b), which developed the essential shared capabilities and focused on social inclusion. These developments attempted to set out a common competency framework that spanned the various disciplines involved in mental health care and unified the professional approaches with a single value based vision. The degree of success, in terms of embedding these developments into practice, appears to be limited, and although some organisations embraced them, others have retained a more traditional uniprofessional or medically dominant approach.

The shared value base

Mental health practice should recognise the rights and aspirations of service users and their families. Practitioners should respond to the needs of people in an honest, non-judgemental and open manner, and:

- provide holistic, needs-led services that take account of the physical, psychological, emotional, social and spiritual needs of individuals and groups;

- conduct legal, ethical and accountable practice and remain open to scrutiny;

- demonstrate a commitment to equality and diversity principles;

- encourage self-determination and freedom of choice.

(Adapted from Hope, 2004 and SCMH, 2001)

The shared value base was not intended to replace the professional Codes of Ethics and Practice of differing professions, but rather to bring them together to create a common ground on which to base multidisciplinary practice. Each professional group will be able to apply their own Code of Practice to this shared vision, a perspective that is embedded within all the professions, policies and legal frameworks that guide and shape the mental health system. One interesting development of note is the establishment of joint professional training – this has been trialled in a small number of universities, with both nursing and social work students undertaking the same training courses, or where an individual undertakes one course, to obtain both the nursing and social work qualifications concurrently. This development could reinforce shared values and competencies, but it also has the potential to dilute professional approaches and must be carefully considered and evaluated.

It should be noted that this is a set of principles on which service delivery should be based, but paternalistic and risk-averse practice can still be found in mental health care. In situations where user rights or wishes are a secondary consideration the role of the practitioner is to challenge these practices and advocate for the individual's rights.

The impact of the recovery approach on the professional value base

The shift in service ethos is linked with the move towards a value based approach and the recovery model has had a significant impact on this. The recovery model has been widely adopted, with its philosophy running through the majority of policy developments over the last decade.

The approach is focused on the individual journey through mental distress, and is based on the principles of hope, self-efficacy, personal dignity, self-determination and person-centredness. One definition, which has been particularly influential, was offered by Anthony in 1993, who stated that recovery was:

> . . . *a deeply personal, unique process of changing one's attitudes, values, feelings, goals, skills and/or roles. It is a way of living a satisfying, hopeful, and contributing life even with limitations caused by the illness. Recovery involves the development of new meaning and purpose in one's life as one grows beyond the catastrophic effects of mental illness.*

(Anthony, 1993, p.17)

Adopting this type of approach required a culture shift across the system, and paternalistic approaches have increasingly been challenged. Services have had to become more person-centred and rights-based (DoH, 2008a), and professional competence has developed according to a common framework for standards and ethics in practice.

Principles of the recovery approach

- The service user directs their own recovery.
- Mental health services must be aware of, and actively work towards addressing dependency.
- Users of service are able to recover more quickly when their:
  - hope is encouraged, enhanced and/or maintained;
  - life roles include a meaningful occupation;
  - spirituality is considered;
  - culture is understood;
  - educational needs as well as those of families/significant others are identified;
  - socialisation needs are identified;
  - they are supported to identify and achieve their goals.
- Individual differences are considered and valued across the life span.
- Recovery is most likely when a holistic approach is considered.
- In order to reflect current 'best practices' there is a need for an integrated approach to treatment and care that includes medical/biological, psychological, social and value-based approaches.
- Practitioners support and promote 'hope'.
- Trusting relationships are developed between workers and service users.
- Practitioners should operate from a strengths/assets model, not focus solely on illness.
- Service users are supported to develop their own recovery plan.

- Friends, families and carers are involved, as defined by the service user.

- Mental health services are most effective when delivery is within the context of the service user's locality and cultural context.

- Community involvement as defined by the user of service is central to the recovery process.

The recovery model is a person-centred approach that emphasises quality of life and experience. This is consistent with the social model and is a way of viewing the person holistically and in their social context. Social work values, and more recently mental health professional values, including AMHP's, reflect this philosophy, and values and ethics now tend to focus on the rights and aspirations of service users.

As a result of the implementation of recovery approaches, social recovery, as well as symptom treatment and management, is becoming a more common practice consideration for professionals working in mental health settings. This type of approach is embedded within the social models of disability that developed from the civil and disability rights movements (Jacobson and Curtis, 2000; Chamberlin, 1990). As a result, although the social work value base has developed over time in direct proportion to the pervading social values of the time, these have also been reflected by and integrated into the basic values of multidisciplinary and interdisciplinary practice in contemporary mental health care.

REFLECTION POINT

- *Considering the values you identified in the previous reflection point, how do these relate to the principles underpinning the recovery approach?*

Working within a recovery approach requires the practitioner to suspend their own beliefs and values in deference to the service user's beliefs and values, and to work with the individual towards the goals they have set for themselves. Being able to analyse personal values and consider how these can support the approach is a reflective exercise that practitioners need to apply. Considering professional responses to risk, or behaviours outside social norms and expectations, is one way in which practitioners can analyse the impact of their own values on their decision making, and assess the influence this can have on an individual's recovery journey. One further comment of note is that a comparison is often made between recovery and the social approach. Although the two approaches have many similarities there are also differences that should be acknowledged. These include the recovery approach's acknowledgement of the more biological and psychological aspects of mental health, and also a central emphasis on the recovery journey, which is not linear in nature and which includes many individual elements that may not always be considered within the traditional social approaches, which see mental illness as a product of the social situation and environmental disabling factors.

CASE STUDY *1.1*

Elaine has been in and out of mental health services for the past five years; she has a care coordinator in the community and has had several admissions to the acute hospital. Her psychiatrist sees her on a bimonthly basis and has prescribed a number of medications, but Elaine feels the side effects of these are worse than the symptoms they are meant to control. Elaine has a diagnosis of schizophrenia but does not agree with this. She has previously received talking therapy in the form of cognitive behavioural therapy (CBT), and has found self-help books useful.

Before becoming ill Elaine was an accountant at a local firm; she gave up her job when she was admitted to hospital for the first time, as she felt unable to continue. She has been claiming benefits ever since, but says she feels as if she has no purpose now.

Elaine is 32 years old; she is single and has a brother, who lives nearby; she stays in contact with one of her friends from college, but does not like to go out much as she feels people are judging her and talking about her behind her back. Before her illness she enjoyed live music and learnt to play the piano; she also used to provide individual tuition for students in basic skills.

ACTIVITY *1.1*

- *What skills, strengths and resources does Elaine have to support her recovery? What are the potential barriers that she may face?*

- *How would Elaine's treatment differ if she was to receive a more traditional service?*

Comment

Within a recovery approach both strengths and needs should be considered, and the resources available to the individual, which include personal interests, informal support networks and the person's aspirations for their recovery all need to be considered. Identifying barriers is also a useful exercise, as this can facilitate better planning and increase the individual's awareness of their own situation. There are differences in how an individual is approached by treatment services: for example, the reluctance to take medication can be planned around in a recovery framework, with self-management and individual choices being considered, whereas in a more traditional approach this reluctance may be seen as an issue of engagement, motivation and compliance.

Personalisation and professional values

There have been significant changes in the delivery of health and social care over the last five years, with user choice and control becoming the main focus of service delivery (DoH, 2007c). Personalisation is an agenda that is being implemented across social care, and health care is likely to follow soon (Darzi, 2008), with individual and personal budgets being provided rather than the more traditional, one-size fits all service models.

The personalisation agenda is a cross-governmental strategy for social care delivery, and in mental health services the uptake has been low. Initiatives such as direct payments are examples of service user choice and control in how they receive social care services. These have been available for almost a decade, and mental health services are significantly underrepresented in their use (CSIP, 2006). The approach has been further developed and expanded into mechanisms such as personal and individual budgets, which service users are allocated to purchase their own support in a way that suits them, and local authorities are required to implement this model across all their service areas. In terms of the implementation process mental health services are still a long way behind other service user groups, and there is anxiety and reticence from professionals about the approach.

There are several reasons why personalisation, and the full-scale implementation of the model of choice and control, is struggling to become embedded in mental health care. These include the differences in how health and social care services are delivered, which for integrated services can be problematic when such a significant service change in one area is required (Bogg, 2008). Public and professional anxiety about the management of risk is another area that is affecting the implementation process. The paternalistic view of service users requiring protection and public perceptions of the dangerousness of mental health issues both contribute to risk-averse practice, and whereas positive risk is advocated as a valid recovery tool (Morgan, 2000; 2007a; 2007b) service culture remains concerned and unwilling to embrace the approach.

For social work the personalised approach is consistent with its theoretical basis of self-determination and social welfare. Whereas workers are anxious about the transformation that is occurring in public services, and what this means for their professional roles, there is not a value conflict to be negotiated as a rights- and strength-based approach is embedded within the profession as a whole. For other professional groups the personalisation of services and the high level of user direction may be more of a culture shift, and although the underpinning professional values are consistent with the approach, the delivery of services in this context will be a challenge to how professionals view their roles and duties. Issues around risk, safeguarding and the use of formal powers do need to be reconciled with the personalisation agenda for all disciplines, and practitioners will be required to develop their competence in terms of maximising the self-efficacy of the individual while ensuring safety.

Issues of power are particularly relevant to this discussion, as the traditional professional powers are becoming increasingly corroded. This is a positive step forward in terms of user empowerment and self-determination; however, as a result professionals will need to balance an increasingly complex power dynamic within their practice.

REFLECTION POINT

- *What does the personalisation of mental health services mean to your practice?*
- *What are the anxieties or concerns you have and what are these based on?*

Comment

Professional values are often a combination of empowerment and protection, and a shift in this dynamic can be anxiety provoking for the practitioner. Personalisation is an approach that rests on service user self-determination, and although this is consistent with the value base it is not always a reflection of how services are actually delivered. Risk aversion is common in mental health environments, and the practitioner's competence in risk assessment and management will need to shift to supporting protective factors and strengths, and better contingency planning in partnership with the individual.

Statutory roles and values

The approved mental health professional (AMHP) and best interest assessor (BIA) roles both require practitioners to apply the core values, and balance risk, in order to make decisions and either make recommendations or directly apply formal measures.

The AMHP role, which in 2008 replaced the approved social worker (ASW) according to the Mental Health Act 2007, has traditionally held the dual role of empowerment and protection, and has concentrated on the ethical use of power in situations that require individual or community protection to be applied. This is governed by a set of guiding principles (DoH, 2008a) that are essentially value statements that the practitioner considers within their decision-making processes. There is an explicit emphasis within AMHP practice on the application of values and the use of powers, and practitioners should be skilled in this approach to practice competently.

For the BIA role, which was introduced under the Deprivation of Liberty Safeguards in 2008 (included in the Mental Health Act 2007 as an amendment to the Mental Capacity Act 2005), the emphasis is slightly different, and the assessment process results in recommendations being made in terms of whether it is in the individual's best interest for a restriction of their liberty to be applied. As with the AMHP, the BIA needs to consider the individual's circumstances in relation to a set of guiding principles (DCA, 2007), which emphasise respect for and the dignity of that individual (see Chapter 10 for further discussion on the capacity legislation and its relationship to human rights issues).

Statutory roles in mental health provision are key examples of the application of value-based practice, as they are governed by human rights and equality considerations while allowing for the application of formal powers that may contravene the wishes of the individual. This can be a difficult balance, and practitioners need to remain aware of the potential impact of their own personal and professional values in the process.

REFLECTION POINT

- *What are the types of behaviour or presentations that are likely to make your decisions more risk-averse?*
- *What is the basis of this response?*

Comment

Practitioners are subject to the same attitudes and beliefs as the rest of society, and although knowledge and skills can alter tolerances to certain situations, the belief system will influence their level of confidence and willingness to take (or not take) a given action. In the case of AMHP and BIA practice, this has significant implications for the individual's liberty, and as such it is vital that practitioners are able to critically analyse their decisions and the basis on which they are made. Recognising and addressing beliefs and prejudices is a core component of ethical practice and should not be underestimated.

Conclusion

This chapter aims to provide a foundation on which to base the rest of this text. Key concepts have been introduced, and the value bases of both social work and mental health practice considered.

Policy developments continue to progress towards empowerment and self-determination, and this is a culture shift for both professionals and services which have traditionally held the power within the system. Multidisciplinary developments and the adoption of recovery approaches have helped to move the focus on mental health services, which are now more inclusive and holistic than before. Shared practice guidance has assisted in the drive towards integrated service provision; however, the different timescales of service transformation are putting pressure on services, and mental health is behind other service user groups in its implementation of personalised care.

Mental health professionals must not only maintain a value base for their practice, but also remain aware of the impact of personal values. Recovery and risk can both be influenced by the attitudes and interventions of practitioners, and critical reflection on their personal beliefs, as well as those of the service user, is a component of ethical practice.

The rest of this book will consider the range of issues that are evident within mental health practice; this includes the development of law and treatment and its interaction with the social context. The principles of human rights are enshrined in the values and ethics of mental health practice, and will be considered in depth. Mental health service users are a diverse group, with a wide range of complex issues; later chapters will focus on some of these issues and explore how practitioners can apply value based and ethical considerations to their practice environments.

Chapter summary

- Values are central to mental health practice for all professional groups.
- Policy developments are consistent with the principles of self-determination and individual rights.

- Upholding an individual's human rights is a fundamental part of practice, and practitioners need to be aware of their duties and reflect upon any interventions within this frame of reference.

- Social work values have developed over time and are reflective of wider social values, an issue that will be explored in more detail in further chapters.

- Mental health professional values continue to be aligned and the shared vision and values encompass social, medical, health and psychological understandings.

FURTHER READING

Hope, R (2004) *The Ten Essential Shared Capabilities – A Framework for the Whole of the Mental Health Workforce.* London: DoH.

SCIE/RCP (2007) *A Common Purpose: Recovery in Future Mental Health Services.* London: SCIE/RCP.

Chapter 2
Ethics, social values and mental health treatment

CHAPTER OBJECTIVES

This chapter will assist readers in meeting the following mental health national occupational standards as relevant to all professional groups, including the statutory roles of AMHP and BIA under mental health and mental capacity legislation.

- A1.1 Reflect on and evaluate your own values, priorities, interests and effectiveness.

- A3 Promote the values and principles underpinning best practice.

Do not fear to be eccentric in opinion, for every opinion now accepted was once eccentric.

Bertrand Russell (1872–1970) British author, mathematician and philosopher

Introduction

Developments in mental health treatment over the past two centuries have been heavily influenced by wider societal understanding and attitudes, and it is possible to identify a direct correlation between how a condition is viewed and the treatment it receives. Early understandings of mental ill health were embedded in religion and superstition (Loschen, 1974; Porter, 2003), with exorcism being the treatment of choice. As western society developed into one of scientific advancement so did the models of treatment and the chemotherapy options, with clinical diagnosis and medical intervention becoming the method of choice.

In the more recent past there has been a strengthening of the disability rights movement and an emergence of social models of disability, which have in turn affected treatment modalities and created a wider acceptance of mental illness. However, this does not mean that prejudice and stigma have disappeared, and there are still significant barriers in terms of how the public regards those who experience mental distress.

As discussed in Chapter 1, the development of a professional value base and ethical framework is rooted in social norms and expectations, and as a result those who present for treatment are subjected to the same wider social attitudes from the professionals tasked to provide services, albeit in a more politically correct form. The formation of societal values is a complex issue based on the full range of socioeconomic and political issues as well as wider global considerations. Ethical decisions are based largely on 'acting in the best interests' of both the individual and the society, or 'doing the right thing'; however, in this context it is necessary to ask who defines what is best and what is right?

Two branches of ethical theory are evident in psychiatric practice: deontology, which emphasises the course of action taken as the major consideration, regardless of the outcome, and teleology, which emphasises the outcome as the most important factor determining whether an action is right or wrong (Macdonald and Beck-Dudley, 1994; Bloch and Green, 2006). Both of these strands can be seen in the history and development of ethical practice within mental health. There remains a philosophical debate with regard to most psychiatric treatment, and this will be explored further in this chapter.

The overall aim of this chapter is to consider the ethics of mental health treatment in the context of the wider social values and to explore the connection between the two areas. How this relationship affects the professional's value base and overall decision making is an important consideration for practitioners, especially when considering the human rights of individuals within the treatment system. No profession that involves working with people can take place in a vacuum, and so the way certain conditions are approached needs to be considered within the wider context of social structures, norms, values and ethics. Social values are defined largely by what society is able to tolerate in terms of risk and behaviour. This is a dynamic concept that has changed throughout history; as such, the level of compulsion placed upon individuals, and the consideration of individual wishes and experiences, now receives more emphasis than before. Despite this, there is still a range of preconceived ideas and beliefs attached to mental health difficulties, and the weight placed upon individual experience can vary, with different ethical considerations being based on what society can tolerate in terms of both the consequences of the treatment modality and the risks and presentation of the individual's mental health condition.

Ethical perspectives

As already mentioned, the two main schools of thought in mental health practice are deontology and teleology. It is useful to set out the framework of these approaches prior to exploring their place within mental health practice.

Ethical practice in most fields follows several key principles, based upon the premise that any intervention must:

- Be appropriate to the presenting problem.
- Be beneficial to the person receiving the intervention.
- Take account of individual autonomy.
- Be socially just, in that its benefits and outcomes can be generalised to the wider society.

(Lolas, 2006; Robertson and Walter, 2007)

Psychiatry and mental health practice applies these principles, but the benefits, social fit and concept of autonomy within this field are not as concrete as in other branches of medicine or human sciences. The development of treatment and the social views of mental health problems will demonstrate this in more depth; however, at this point it is useful to begin to think about mental health interventions from a perspective that allows for compulsory treatment and detention based on professionally assessed risk to both self and others regardless of the individual's view; this in itself allows for the erosion of personal autonomy in a way that other disciplines would find unacceptable.

Teleology is a branch of ethics that emphasises the final outcomes of any intervention. This school of thought is aligned to utilitarian approaches, whereby the ultimate benefit is the most important consideration; however, the duty to the patient or service user adds a dimension that is not present in other disciplines (Hare, 1993). Interventions such as electroconvulsive therapy (ECT) could be considered to be teleological. The interventions themselves can be difficult and at times traumatic for the patient; however, the practitioner is seen to have a duty to the individual under their care, and as such, although the action is against the individual's wishes, or may cause short-term difficulties (for example memory loss in the case of ECT), it may still be considered ethical as there is a high likelihood of a beneficial outcome for certain patients (remission rates 87%+ in some conditions; Petrides et al., 2001). The criticisms associated with this approach are the lack of an absolute or certain outcome; the causes of mental illness are still largely undetermined; and although some people respond to some treatments this is not sufficiently concrete or quantifiable to state that the morality of the approach is irrelevant, as the outcomes are definitely good (Bloch and Green, 2006; Robertson and Walter, 2007).

Deontology, on the other hand, applies the principle that the actions are equally as important as the outcome. This approach is embedded within the philosophy defined by Kant (1983 edition), who suggested that ethics should be grounded on duty and morality, and that practitioners should do the right thing based on their moral duty as both an individual and a professional (Bloch and Green, 2006). For example, a practitioner could refrain from treating an individual with forced medication against their will because of the short-term trauma and stress it might cause, and because the challenge to the individual's autonomy could not be reconciled with the practitioner's own value base. The criticism levelled at this approach in mental health practice is that the individual may not always be able to make an informed and rational decision regarding their own treatment, and the refusal to comply with professionally defined regimens at a specific period in time could have a detrimental impact upon their long-term condition and recovery.

As illustrated, both approaches attract criticism, and the nature of mental illness – from both an individual and a social perspective – means that there are very few objective measures available to inform the alliance of professional groups to either branch of ethical thought. Ethical practice, in the majority of cases, is applied to a set of values that enable practitioners to act in the interests of the individual and the wider society in a manner that is the least restrictive available, and although philosophical debates will continue, there are no hard and fast rules with regard to which perspective is best.

James is a 23-year-old man who lives alone in a bedsit in a city centre. His family live 200 miles away, and his contact with them is very limited – occasional phone calls only. James was diagnosed with schizophrenia 4 years ago following an admission to the local psychiatric unit, presenting with psychotic symptoms. He has since had a further five admissions, on each occasion reporting hearing voices and believing that his neighbours and the support team are trying to hurt him.

James admits to using heroin, cocaine and cannabis on a regular basis, and he is physically dependent on heroin. He is well known to both the local CMHT and the drug services, but states that he does not want to stop using drugs as they are the only relief he gets from the negative voices that he hears, telling him to harm himself. He is prescribed antipsychotic medication but does not take it, as he says it makes him feel strange and as if he can't think properly. He has recently been readmitted to the inpatient unit as he was found by the police in a distressed state and brought in on a section 136 of the Mental Health Act 1983 (as amended by MHA 2007); he was assessed and is now detained under section 3. His consultant psychiatrist wants to change his medication to a two-weekly injection to make sure James takes it; he also wants to conduct an opiate detoxification while James is under section on the unit.

James has the capacity to make decisions about his medication and does not want injections. He does not want to take medication, and is aware that when he does not take it he becomes unwell; nor does he want to undergo opiate detoxification.

- *What are the teleological and deontological considerations in this case?*
- *In your practice, which approach would fit best with your own professional and/or individual values? Consider why this is the case.*

Comment

Both ethical approaches are evident within this case study and the practitioner will need to consider both schools of thought. Teleological approaches are evident in issues such as compulsory treatment and detention in hospital, whereas deontological approaches can be seen in the choices that James is enabled to make.

The reality of mental health practice is that a range of ethical perspectives could be applied, often interchangeably. The varied nature of both the service user groups and the range of disciplines, combined with the varied and dynamic nature of social values and approaches, means that no one school of thought can be consistently applied. Advances in both models of treatment and societal understandings of mental illness have further diluted the adherence to any one approach, and the complexity of legal sanctions for those presenting with high-risk behaviours means that although the commitment to a morality of approach is evident, it is not always possible to take account of the key principles of autonomy, individual benefit and social benefit within the same treatment episode. The task of the practitioner is therefore to apply the values of acting in an individual's best interest and weighing this against societal interest as a core part of the decision-making process. This is a difficult task and one that should not be underestimated.

The rest of this chapter seeks to set out the historical developments in mental health treatment in an attempt to show the links with the development of social values. Mental health is a field that, more than any other human science or medical discipline, is linked to social context, and the social construct of ethical frameworks is apparent throughout the history of psychiatry and mental health practice.

Historical development of treatment and social view of mental illness

The treatment for mental distress, and indeed what is considered effective and ethical, has developed throughout history. The way that mental illness is understood and approached has changed from the first documented accounts, where mental illnesses, especially psychotic traits, were considered supernatural in origin (Loschen, 1974; Carson, 1973; Boehnlein, 2000), through to more recent emphasis on medical intervention and social inclusion. As understanding has changed, so have the modes of treatment, creating a dimension within the ethical debate concerning whether such debates are less about what is right and more about what is acceptable (Cottone, 2001; Chaloner, 1999).

At those periods in history where the supernatural was largely used to explain symptoms, there was an emphasis on demonology and possession, using interventions such as exorcism and spiritual healing as the main methods of treatment. Although the understanding remains that the spiritual dimension of an individual is important to overall well-being, these approaches are no longer viewed as either effective or ethical by the majority of society or the professionals involved. The view that spirit possession was the cause of mental distress was rooted in societal beliefs that emphasised superstition and folklore as central to understanding both the environment and the human condition. Medical or scientific explanations had not yet been discovered or developed, and communities had strong affiliations to religious organisations, with churches wielding significant power in society (Loschen, 1974; Koenig, 2005; Boehnlein, 2000).

Different spiritual beliefs led to various methods of understanding and dealing with mental distress, and as a result approaches in the Islamic world began to separate from those of Christianity. The Muslim world's adherence to the Qu'ran, for example, led to an approach to mental illness that was more sympathetic than that of Christianity, seeing those experiencing symptoms as in need of care and requiring a guardian. This approach led to the establishment of the some of the earliest asylums (Boehnlein, 2000; Jain, 2003; Carlson, 1973) for the treatment of mental illness; similar examples are documented in Buddhist countries (Boehnlein, 2000; Koenig, 2005).

As scientific advancement progressed, social beliefs began to shift and the emphasis on spiritual and religious explanations lessened. The western world's fear of mental illness led to an approach of containment and treatment; however, there was no scientific approach to treatment, and although the first asylums in Europe were established in the 13th century, these were custodial in nature and no efficacy was evident (Shorter, 1997; Porter, 2003).

The emphasis on asylums continued over the next three centuries, with small numbers of individuals, deemed to be 'lunatics', confined within them. The conditions in these establishments were universally poor and regimes often brutal, degradation and unsanitary environments being the norm (Brimblecombe, 2006; Shorter, 1997; Coleborn, 2001). Those considered dangerous were often manacled and chained to the walls and floors; the historian Roy Porter called the history of Bethlem Hospital in the UK:

> . . . *a symbol for man's inhumanity to man, for callousness and cruelty.*

(Olden, 2003; 22)

During the 18th century people used to go to Bethlem to view the lunatics. For a penny, members of the public could look into their cells and view what became known as the 'show of Bethlem', which was generally of a sexual nature or violent fights. It is speculated that on the first Tuesday of the month entry was free, and it is thought that up to 96,000 people may have participated each year, although there is limited objective evidence to support these speculations (Andrews et al., 1997).

Moral weakness was a common diagnosis at this point in psychiatric history, and was one reason why such treatment of those considered mad was justified by society: those who experienced madness were considered to have lived immoral lives that must have led to their symptoms, and as such were not fit to live in the wider community (Szasz, 1961; Neff and Husaini, 1985). This view can still be observed in relation to a commonly held public perception of people with drug and alcohol addictions.

From a teleological perspective the asylum culture could be considered ethical at this time, as it provided an outcome that was considered necessary by wider society, i.e. social segregation. Whereas today this acceptance would be considered unethical, at the time the understanding of mental distress was that it required containment. Treatments that were humane and effective had yet to be developed, and as a result the asylum caretakers were tasked to provide a social service, i.e. protecting the wider community from those who presented a risk to social order.

By the late 18th century medical practitioners were seriously questioning the principle of containment. In 1758, English physician William Battie wrote his *Treatise on Madness*, which called for treatments to be used. This was the first significant English contribution to the field of psychiatry and advocated an optimistic view of the treatability of insanity by the management of symptoms. Battie's view gained support when, 30 years later, King George III became known to be suffering from a mental disorder. Following the King's remission in 1789, mental illness began to be seen as something that could be treated and cured (Kendell, 2001).

This development went against the previous view that madness was a moral weakness, and also called into question the acceptability of cruelty and the ethics of ridicule and incarceration – if the king, a man who was born to rule, could be affected, what did that say about the causes and nature of mental illness?

Battie's writings can be seen as a turning point in the medical approach to mental illness, and his promotion of therapeutic optimism through engagement with the patient, rather than restraint and other physical tortures, led to the development of the more humane and so-called 'moral' therapy that was later to be provided at the York Retreat. This development did not end the use of treatments that by today's standards would be seen as unethical. Methods of treatment over the next century included psychosurgery, fever treatments, continuous bathing and enemas. Widespread use of psychosurgery, which caused significant personality changes and irreversible cognitive damage, was an accepted form of treatment until the 1960s, as characterised in Ken Kesey's 1962 novel *One Flew Over the Cuckoo's Nest*. In 1949, Antonio Egas Moniz, the surgeon who pioneered lobotomy as a treatment for schizophrenia, was awarded a Nobel prize for his work. In today's society to recommend lobotomy as a treatment option is not just ethically questionable, it is also abhorrent, and as such demonstrates the direct linkage between ethics and social acceptability.

REFLECTION POINT

- *What emphasis is placed on cultural and spiritual understandings of mental distress both in your local area and in your practice? Why is this?*

Comment

Cultural and spiritual understandings form a core part of the individual belief system, defining what is acceptable and what we are willing to tolerate in terms of behavioural norms and overall risk taking. The practitioner needs to remain aware of their own belief systems, and hence their own understanding, to mitigate the impact of their own levels of tolerance.

Social tolerance to both mental illness and risk is an important point; in this discussion we have seen an evolution throughout the history of the treatment of mental illness that has matched the social understanding of what it means, and this is embedded within the changes in both social culture and the influence of religion and spiritual belief. What is acceptable behaviour is a dynamic issue, and mental health care has changed as a result; this can also be seen in other areas, for example the role of women and that of disabled groups in society. Class is one further example, and one that has influenced the development of mental health care and treatment. Whereas mental health problems were previously seen as a lower-class weakness, they are now recognised as crossing class boundaries, and as a result society has become more tolerant and accepting.

Social class and mental illness

Social class has had an impact on how mental illness is both viewed and experienced, and as such must be considered within this debate. There is a double impact that needs to be considered in this context: first, the impact of social class and social exclusion on the development of mental illness; and second, how these factors compound difficulties and create barriers to recovery.

The majority of the 'lunacy' developments over the 19th and 20th centuries were rooted in the Poor Laws, with workhouses established alongside asylums to house those who were considered unable to live within mainstream society due to illness and disability, but who did not have the means to support themselves. The correlation between deprivation, poverty and the incidence of mental ill health is now well established (Hudson, 2005; Weich and Lewis, 1998; Ritsher et al., 2001); however, in previous years the presumption that the lower classes were morally corrupt or weak was the pervading view, and these individuals were seen as needing to be locked away to protect the general public. Conversely, those in the upper or upper middle classes who experienced symptoms of mental illness, and were of sufficient means or social standing, were often seen as eccentric or in need of help from physicians or clerics, King George III being one such example.

The reality of living in poverty makes the experience of mental distress all the more difficult. When an individual has little or no social or economic support the level of distress is often more acute. Although this is also the case with physical health difficulties, pressures such as inability to pay bills, and a lower level of education, can often result in greater inequalities between the individual and the professional. Added to this, a lack of stable housing or occupational activity all serve to compound the individual's feelings of worthlessness, hopelessness and helplessness – all factors that research has shown can contribute to increased levels of distress (Vanfossen et al., 1981; Tew, 2007; Hudson, 2005; Weich and Lewis, 1998) and a poorer long-term prognosis.

REFLECTION POINT

- *What is the impact of social and economic factors on the recovery of the service users and carers you have contact with in your day-to-day practice?*

- *Can you think of examples where such factors (or lack of them) have affected your decision making?*

Comment

The impact of socioeconomic influences is an area that warrants a much more lengthy discussion than that presented here, and there are a great many texts on the subject; however, the context in which a decision is made links directly to the values and beliefs of the decision maker, social tolerance of mental health issues, and the risks presented to both the individual and society.

These divisions in individual experience and the methods of treatment, which were based on socioeconomic status, were extensively debated by sociological theorists such as Marx and Durkheim, both of whom proposed a understanding that saw psychiatric treatment as a form of social control rather than a medical discipline (Bastide, 1972; Steadman, 1972;

Cohen, 1985; Nahem, 1982), an argument that gained momentum and formed the basis of the anti-psychiatry movement.

Anti-psychiatry as a social commentary

Anti-psychiatry, which was an understanding developed in the 1960s and 1970s, had a significant role in the development of modern mental health practice and to a certain extent assisted in redefining the role of psychiatry. The 1960s heralded a level of scrutiny that had not previously been present within mental health care, with prominent commentators such as Laing and Szasz questioning the power base of medical psychiatry (Laing, 1960; Szasz, 1972), and increasing criticism from survivor groups concerning what were considered breaches of human rights and abuses of power by the professionals involved (Hopton, 2006; Double, 2006; Rogers and Pilgrim, 1991).

The 1960s and 1970s were two decades of significant global social change, reforms including an increased emphasis on civil rights, women entering the labour market on a competitive basis, and a heightened awareness of social problems and political changes (Jenkins, 1983; So, 1990; McMichael, 2004). The anti-psychiatry and survivor movements were part of this socioeconomic context, and reflected the thinking of the times. However, since then the level of criticism has reduced and the anti-psychiatry movement has softened into critical psychiatry (Double, 2006), but this period signalled the start of significant changes throughout the mental health and disability rights fields, which can still be seen in modern service and policy drivers. Although the mental health professions could argue that social control was a legitimate function of their role, the emphasis on the process and deontology approaches at this time meant that this was no longer sufficient justification for the methods of psychiatric care, and these challenges resulted in a reform of mental health practice across all of the disciplines.

The development of the social work role

Throughout the 20th century huge advances were made in the treatment of mental health problems, with medical advancements leading to more comprehensive categorisation and diagnosis of conditions and pharmaceutical developments for symptom control. The diagnostic systems developed by Kraepelin (1906) and his successors form the foundations for the DSM and ICD classification systems that are still in use today. The work of Freud (1965) and other psychoanalytical psychiatrists around this time significantly influenced the development of psychotherapeutic approaches that are still in common use.

Although the environments and treatments in asylums were by today's standards barbaric, inhumane and unethical, they did provide a platform for the development of psychiatry. Like many scientific developments, psychiatry has a dark past, rooted in superstition and containment (Shorter, 1997; Porter and Michale, 1994); however, access to many individuals, experiencing myriad symptoms and conditions, provided practitioners with a captive audience on whom trials of treatments and advancements could be practised.

Parallel developments to these can be seen in social work. Charity and welfare models, consistent with the dominant social values of the times, developed into a professional approach based on the value of the individual and the negotiation of social structures and relationships as a core part of its purpose (Brandon et al., 1995; Bisman, 2003). As discussed in Chapter 1, social work has its roots in charitable organisations and welfare principles; however, in the early 1900s psychiatric social work was established as a profession in the asylum setting. As with medical psychiatry, the approach had developed throughout history, moving through morality and religious considerations (Leiby, 1984) through to a more objective application of values and into the level of evidence-based practice and professionalism that can be seen today (Reamer, 2006).

Contemporary understandings: the impact of roles and guidelines

It has already been noted that both teleological and deontological perspectives are evident within the field of mental health, and which of these is applied changes according to social context, social tolerance of behaviour and the level of perceived risk. It is also notable that role has an impact on which school of ethical thought is applied. In the main service user groups apply deontology, with the means being just as important as the outcome. This is understandable, given the experiences that are common in mental health. Service user research and involvement have further strengthened the view, and the concepts of choice and control which are not embedded within the policy direction will continue this emphasis. However, despite this it appears that the legislative framework and the clinical guidelines such as those produced by the National Institute of Clinical Excellence (NICE) remain teleological in nature, and emphasise the outcome rather than the journey.

The differences in the perspectives are not surprising, as in each role the focus is different. For those developing the guidelines the emphasis is on the efficacy of the treatment provided, with a basic question being 'what works?'. If the outcome of treatments such as ECT, medication or cognitive behavioural therapy (CBT) is that there is a reduction in symptoms of mental illness, then they are considered efficacious and hence ethical and recommended for use within the treatment system; although the experience of users is considered, the overall aim is to treat and cure, and as such the end justifies the means. The emphases on user experience in the literature are evident; however, in the main NICE guidelines retain a focus on outcomes, and in health services in particular, compliance with these guidelines is a service requirement.

For service users and carers the emphasis is more about the experience or journey: what the treatment feels like at the time is important, and negative experiences are often avoided despite what the outcome may be; examples of this can be seen in medication compliance: the outcome of complying with medication may be an improvement in overall symptoms, but the side effects of the medication may be such that the individual will choose to not engage with the treatment regimen regardless of the possible benefits – a phenomenon not confined to mental health.

Roles such as the AMHP stand on the crossroads between teleological and deontological approaches, and hence conflicts can occur. The compulsory treatment of an individual who is resisting, but for whom the outcome may be beneficial if treatment is applied, is a teleological consideration; however, the role is to consider the whole circumstance and take account of the individual's views and wishes, which will largely be to resist compulsion. This creates a conflict within the practitioner's decision making: do they exercise protection of the individual and public by applying compulsion, or do they adhere to the patient's experience and wishes by resisting? Both of these actions have consequences, and there is a need for the practitioner to consider these in their assessment and decision-making processes.

Contemporary understandings, stigma and the impact on the individual

The historical development of treatment for mental illness clearly demonstrates that societal views have had a significant impact upon the way those experiencing mental distress are treated. Within modern service provision there is an increasing emphasis on user involvement and participation (Beresford, 2006; Pilgrim and Waldron, 1998; Munro et al., 2006; Glasby and Beresford, 2006; Rush, 2004) and recognition of the importance of user and carer experiences and expertise in improving and developing services.

Research evidence in relation to the impact of stigma has received attention over recent years, and a number of anti-stigma campaigns have been launched as a result. There is now more of an acknowledgement that mental health issues can affect anyone at any time; however, there is still a substantial body of evidence indicating that discrimination and stigmatisation are still a barrier to social inclusion and an issue in terms of the promotion of recovery (SEU, 2003; Sayce, 2001; Sayce and Measley, 1999; Pinfold et al., 2005; Schneider and Bramley, 2008; Morgan et al., 2007; Curran et al., 2007).

The modern understanding of mental illness is based on empirical evidence that biological, sociological and psychological factors all play a part in an individual's level of mental health, and the recovery model, based on a holistic view of all of these elements, is now widely embraced. However, the objective understanding of mental distress is not always reconciled with the approach of others to those experiencing difficulties: for example, in some research studies mental health professionals are cited as contributing to the experience of stigma, by labelling those they are trying to help (Hugo, 2001; Corrigan, 2004; Nordt et al., 2005). In some instances service users may be labelled as unable to participate in certain activities, either because of their perceived inabilities or the potential risks they present, and hence are not supported to access the full range of resources available to them – direct payments are an example of this, with mental health showing the lowest uptake of the facility owing to workers' reluctance to 'take a risk' with service users (Ridley and Jones, 2003; Spandler, 2004).

REFLECTION POINT

Considering your own practice and caseload:

- *What type of activities can be supported by the use of direct payments/individual budgets?*

- *What is your experience of direct payments/individual budgets? If you have no experience of these areas, ask your colleagues who have facilitated access to these facilities – what are the benefits and potential risks of the approach?*

Comment

The social view of what it means to be mentally ill has a far-reaching influence on the practitioner, and service users are often seen as needing protection rather than empowerment. Although practitioners are required to exercise reflective practice and examine their own values, many of these are ingrained and unconscious, based on what is socially acceptable.

Service users can be empowered to make choices and exercise control via initiatives such as direct payments: ethically, the freedom to take the risks involved in such areas is entrenched within the teleological theory – the outcome justifies the means; however, in mental health, deontological thought would suggest that the means is as important as the end result; it can therefore be suggested that the reluctance of practitioners to engage with such initiatives is due to a protectionist point of view.

Perceived capacity is another area that can prevent individuals participating in and contributing to wider societal activity. The presumption that an individual suffering from severe mental illness does not have the capacity to take on certain tasks is common, both within professional groups and within wider society, and as such access to socioeconomic opportunities, such as employment and community involvement, can be restricted. Employers, for example, need information and support to understand and engage with mental health issues, and although the government has legislated against discrimination in the form of the Disability Discrimination Act, this is not enough to change attitudes and negative images of mental illness. As a result, mental health service users experience many barriers in terms of social involvement and the stigma of mental illness. This includes aspects such as the fear of violence, lack of support, and presumptions about their ability (Corrigan, 2007; Griffiths, 2001). These views are embedded in society and can significantly affect an individual's experience and the outcomes of treatment.

REFLECTION POINT

- *What words and images do you immediately think of when you hear the following terms?*

Drug addict	*Prostitute*
Social worker	*Teenage mother*
Feminist	*Politician*
Paranoid schizophrenia	*Christian*
Psychiatrist	*Transsexual*
Depressed	*Student*
Businessman	*Musician*

- *What is the impact of these labels on the way you approach an individual?*

The aim of this exercise is to demonstrate the connotations of different labels. Different value systems will place different meanings on each label: this is not restricted to mental health, but is rather a wider phenomenon linked to overall social beliefs. Examples are seen throughout society, and the practitioner needs to consider them within their own practice.

Conclusion

This chapter has considered a range of issues, ranging from the ethical framework of interventions through to the historical and contemporary views of mental illness and links to social values and understandings of mental distress.

Ethical perspectives are an important part of mental health practice and the practitioner needs to have an overview of the issues. It is difficult to attempt to place mental health within a specific school of ethical thought, as these change according to treatment modality, role, social values and norms, as well as the level of perceived or actual risk. As such, an emphasis on the values that relate to the best interests of both the individual and society, and the possible effectiveness of any given approach, are the cornerstones of ethics in this context.

Interventions and treatment models in the mental health field have seen significant developments and reforms over the last century, and these can be mapped to changes and advances in society. Throughout history there is evidence of this linkage – whether this be the establishment of asylums in the 18th and 19th centuries, where containment was considered necessary as a way of protecting communities from threat, or the reform of the 1960s and 1970s when disability rights came to the forefront of people's minds and equality and efficacy of treatment became the emphasis.

The current situation that is influencing mental health practice is the emphasis on clinical effectiveness and person-centred care. Although stigma remains a key barrier to recovery from mental illness, treatment advances continue and the advocacy- and rights-based approaches that are more consistent with deontology are evident in most areas of voluntary treatment.

Despite the advances in our understanding of mental health issues, and the recognition that one in four of the UK population will suffer from some form of mental distress at some point in their lives, there remains a level of stigma and prejudice within society that continues to significantly affect the social interaction and experience of both those experiencing mental distress and the wider community. Media influences play a large part in this situation, along with the use of labels that have negative connotations.

In the context of mental health practice there is a need to explore the practitioner's individual and professional values, ensuring that prejudices are acknowledged and challenged rather than ignored. Practitioners are people, and as such are as susceptible to wider social values as anyone else. Knowledge of a situation does not necessarily result in a change in attitude or behaviour, and the reflective processes – whether as part of continuing professional development or regular supervision – need to be embedded in the practice environment.

Chapter summary

- This chapter has explored the historical development of mental health care and considered the dynamic development of social norms, values and tolerances in terms of their impact on how treatment is provided.

- Both deontological and teleological perspectives remain evident within mental health, and aspects such as role, social context and levels of risk continue to influence which branch of ethics is observed.

- The practitioner, especially the AMHP, is often at the crossroads of the two approaches, being required to both empower and protect, and as such must remain aware of their own as well as the service user's context and belief system.

- The AMHP's role is to consider the whole circumstances of each case, and the factors that influence the AMHP's decisions in each situation should also be considered.

- The role of the AMHP is to consider the whole circumstance, and this should include their own decision making.

FURTHER READING

Bloch, S and Green, SA (2006) An ethical framework for psychiatry. *British Journal of Psychiatry*, 188: 7–12.

Shorter, E (1997) *A History of Psychiatry*. Chichester: Wiley.

Chapter 3
The development of mental health law

No law or ordinance is mightier than understanding.

Plato, (428 BC–348 BC) Classical Greek philosopher and mathematician

Introduction

As mental health attitudes and treatment have developed, so too has the legislative framework within which services operate. Mental health law has changed significantly over the last century, in line with the pervading social understandings of mental health issues. As discussed in Chapter 2, the way mental health issues are responded to is very dependent on what is considered ethical, a concept which has continued to develop throughout the history of mental health treatment.

This chapter moves on from the previous discussion and sets out the legislative context within which practitioners operate. This includes both a historical view of how mental health law has developed in the UK, and the role of values and ethics within the current legal frameworks. An overview of the Mental Capacity Act and Mental Health Act will be set out, and the importance of the guiding principles of each will be central to the discussion.

The impact of social values and perceptions as a whole is an important aspect of understanding how legal frameworks are developed, and the aim here is to provide the social and legal context for further discussion. The codes of practice are the vehicles which explicitly link the law and the value base, and these are a direct reflection of how society responds to mental health issues. As such, in order to develop and maintain competence, practitioners dealing with mental health legislation need to be aware of the social contexts and able to consider values and ethics within their application of the law.

The Poor Law and mental health

The origins of the mental health legal framework are set in the context of other legislation introduced to manage poverty and destitution. This chapter does not seek to provide a comprehensive historical account, but rather highlights the key legislative changes and social histories that contribute to the overall discussion of values and ethics in mental health care.

The Poor Law of 1601 was the first major piece of law that required authorities to provide for those who were unable to provide for themselves, and this was funded via local rates and property taxes. Those considered unable to work at this time were referred to as the 'impotent poor', and each local area had to make arrangements for those who were born or settled in that area; those who did not fit these criteria and were unable to work could be expelled from the area. This relief was paid on a scale and administered by 'overseers of the poor', who were unpaid parish members, supervised by the local Justice of the Peace (Hopkins, 1979).

During the 18th century a number of 'Madhouse' and 'Vagrancy' Acts were passed, amended, and later repealed. They related largely to those who were not necessarily destitute, but who were detained in an institution because of mental health issues. The 1714 Vagrancy Act is thought to be the first English statute that provided specifically for the detention of 'lunatics' (Bridge and Bridge, 1984; Bartlett, 1999; Pereira and Dalton, 2006), and in 1774 private madhouses became regulated under the Madhouses Act.

The County Asylum Act of 1808 provided a permissive power to the Justices of each county to build asylums to replace the small provisions in voluntary hospitals that offered psychiatric treatment; however, this development was not embraced at the time, largely because of the financing requirements, which had to be found from local rates and taxes (Hopkins, 1979). At a time when mental distress was understood to be a moral condition, the use of taxes to build asylums and contain those who were unable to live and work in mainstream society was not popular. As a result, many of those who were most unwell were held in jails or lived on the edges of society in extreme poverty and destitution (Pereria and Dalton, 2006; Means and Smith, 1994).

In 1834 the Poor Law was amended as a result of a review undertaken by a Royal Commission on the Poor Laws, which was appointed in 1832 to review the use of poor law provisions across 15,000 parishes in England and Wales. The country's population had increased from 5.5 million to 13.9 million in the first quarter of the 19th century, and the industrial revolution was having a severe impact on the economic situation.

Increased mechanisation stabilised England's self-sufficiency, but led to increases in unemployment, increases in the rate of poverty among the working classes, and civil unrest (Bartlett, 1999; Hopkins, 1979). In this social context reform was the only practical option. The Commission's report was published in 1834 and the amended legislation was passed in the same year. This abolished the system of outdoor (or community) relief that had been introduced by the 1601 Act, and specified that support for those in poverty should be provided only within an institution and according to a set of eligibility criteria. This led to the building of workhouses in each parish to accommodate the poor, the ill, or older people who were not able to support themselves, or who had no relatives they could depend on (Driver, 1993; Hopkins, 1979; Alcock, 1996).

Poor Law relief post 1834

The 1834 Act introduced a system of eligibility; this did not apply to children, who were considered blameless for their situations:

- No able-bodied person was to receive money or other help from the Poor Law authorities except in a workhouse.

- Conditions in workhouses were to be made very harsh to discourage people from wanting to receive help.

- Workhouses were to be built in every parish or, if parishes were too small, in unions of parishes.

The administration of workhouses was also subject to a range of rules, designed to make life in them less desirable:

- The separation of inmates into different categories, including the separation of families and married couples.

- Schools for children and work for the able-bodied.

- Plain but 'sufficient' food, and a ban on tobacco and spirits.

- Separate wards for the sick, including those with mental health problems.

- Wearing of a workhouse uniform, and inmates not being allowed to leave without permission.

The system of parish overseers was also amended, as it was believed that this level of local discretion had led to fraudulent use of the poor funds (Hopkins, 1979; Bartlett, 1999), and a new administration body called 'the union' was created. This moved the management of the workhouses from local Justices of the Peace to a Board of Guardians, who were elected tax payers. As Bartlett (1999) commented, the new Poor Law signalled:

. . . an ideological movement away from the paternalistic notions of the old Poor Law, toward a system of faceless administration imposing moral choices and moral judgements on the poor.

(Bartlett, 1999; p.21)

The management of those with mental health issues was absent from this piece of legislation, with the one exception being that a person considered dangerous could only remain in the workhouse for up to 14 days. As with the 1601 Act, there was a presumption that those considered mentally unwell were included in the 'impotent poor' category (Bartlett, 1999), and would be housed in workhouses, or in some cases the workhouse infirmary.

What are the issues from an ethical perspective of having:

- *An overseer committee of local volunteers?*

- *An elected Board of Governors?*

Comment

The motivations of individuals involved in these systems were likely to be variable, with both philanthropy and political ideologies informing the local systems. Public perception of both poverty and mental health issues were both largely negative at this point in English history, and these attitudes would inform what provisions were made. As discussed in Chapter 2, what is considered ethical is based largely on social norms and expectations, and the conduct and decision making of such committees would be heavily influenced by the pervading social values. Changing the system to an elected board does serve to distance the decision making from the individual somewhat; however, it can also take the humanistic elements out of the process, and as such both systems were essentially flawed, but provided for both positive and negative effects on those within the Poor Law system who had mental health issues.

Asylum legislation

In 1845 the Lunacy Act was passed through parliament; this piece of legislation required county areas to provide asylums, and over the next 25 years a network of large asylums was built throughout England. The Act identified that:

> . . . *lunatics and other insane persons . . . in Gaols, Houses of Correction, Poor Houses and Houses of Industry, is highly dangerous and inconvenient.*

> (Cited in Pereria and Dalton, 2006; p.1)

As well as the social attitudes towards the mentally unwell requiring specific treatment, and increasing social concern about their treatment, these reforms were also supported by the funding arrangements. Unlike the Poor Laws, which placed responsibility on individual parishes to finance the system through local taxation, the asylum act moved this responsibility to county councils, which were largely funded via central taxation, and as a result local parishes were keen to move the local workhouse population into the county asylums and transfer the financial burden to the larger authorities.

Admission to an asylum at this time required certification as *'a lunatic, an idiot or a person of unsound mind'* (Means and Smith, 1994; p.28) and an order to be detained by a judicial authority had to be applied for. By 1890 there were 66 county and borough asylums in England and Wales, housing an average of 802 inmates, and with over 86,000 individuals certified as insane, this was a fourfold increase over a 40-year period (Gibbins, 1988).

One further element of the Lunacy Act is that it also established the Lunacy Commission, a government body responsible for overseeing treatment and conduct within the new system. Whereas the Madhouse Acts of the 1700s had introduced oversight by the Royal College of Physicians, this development was the first formal oversight that was applied by the state to the treatment of mental health conditions (Shaw et al., 2007) and paved the way for the regulatory system as we currently know it. The Lunacy Acts of 1890 and 1891 further built on this regulation, and laws were introduced to regulate asylums and compulsory care and ensure that there was a criterion in place so that only those with the most severe conditions were admitted into hospital.

In 1913 the Board of Control, established under the Mental Deficiency Act, replaced the Lunacy Commission as the regulating body, with extended oversight to include mental deficiency (learning disability) provision, an arrangement that stayed in place until 1959. One of the further developments of the 1913 Act was that it introduced the concept of 'morally defective' and 'feeble minded' to the definition of mental deficiency, which were later highlighted as being applied to people of average intelligence but who behaved unconventionally (Percy, 1957).

Social welfare and mental health

In 1930, the Mental Treatment Act was passed, signifying a shift in attitude within mental health legislation, as admission to an asylum could now be on a voluntary basis and certification was no longer necessary. The certification of insanity was a significant source of social stigma and made it very difficult to exit the asylum system, so this shift to voluntary care signalled a shift in how mental health problems were viewed. Psychiatric advances indicated that outpatient care, aftercare and prevention were effective treatment options, and the legal framework needed to reflect this (Royal Commission, 1926; Moncrieff, 2003).

Significant changes in social welfare occurred during the 1940s, with both the creation of the NHS as a health care service available to all, and the implementation of the National Assistance Act in 1948, which placed a duty on local authorities to provide accommodation for *persons who, by reason of age, illness, disability or any other circumstances, are in need of care and attention which is not otherwise available to them.* The workhouses had closed following the repeal of the Poor Law in 1930, which had transferred the workhouse infirmaries to local authorities, and the establishment of the welfare state represented a significant change in how those with mental health problems were treated.

In the postwar period a culture of welfare reform, and support for those in need began to pervade society, and this included mental health care. The 1959 Mental Health Act was the next significant change. Following the recommendations of the Percy Report (Percy, 1957), which recommended a system in which mental disorder was perceived and treated as a normal health matter, the 1959 Mental Health Act introduced a system which considered compulsory hospital admission as a last resort and made councils responsible for community care (Jones, 1960; BBC, 1999). Under this law safeguards for patients were tightened, including the establishment of Mental Health Review Tribunals (MHRT), replacing the Board of Control, with the responsibility to review detentions. The practice of multidisciplinary assessment was also introduced, with mental welfare officers (MWO) acting as independent practitioners and applicants for admission. A clear definition of mental disorder, and exclusions relating to promiscuity, were also introduced, and the concepts of morality contained in the previous Mental Deficiency Act were abolished.

During the 1960s and 1970s mental health care shifted emphasis from large asylums and hospital settings to outpatient and more localised services. Legislation was introduced to create a more joined-up provision (Local Authorities Act 1970), better services and advances in medical treatment were developed, and the policy of community-based care, which is still in place today, was established.

REFLECTION POINT

- *What are the social implications of such a significant shift in treatment emphasis?*

- *How would this affect ethical practice?*

Comment

The shift from asylum to community care took place in a social context of increasing welfare reforms and an understanding of mental illness that included recognition of difficulties as a health issue. Ethical practice developed into a more socially aware model, and medical advances enabled better outcomes for individuals.

Contemporary legal framework

The Mental Health Act 1983 continued the theme of social welfare, increased individuals' rights and strengthened safeguards. The prevention of admission wherever possible, and the requirement for aftercare were both key factors in this legislation (Barnes et al., 1990; Szmuckler and Holloway, 2000), which mirrored the developments in care, treatment and the strength of the user voice that were characteristic of the time. Definitions were tightened, and further exclusions added in the form of drug and alcohol addiction. Approved social workers replaced mental welfare officers and brought a social perspective to the decision-making process, ensuring that wider circumstances were considered and admission prevented where community alternatives could be used to support the individual and manage the risks.

Following a number of high-profile cases, including the homicides of Jonathan Zito by Christopher Clunis in 1992, and Megan and Lin Russell by Michael Stone in 1996, and the commencement of the 'Bournewood' case (see Chapter 9 for full details) relating to a man who was informally detained and deprived of his liberty, the government was under pressure to reform a system that was seen as flawed and lacking in protection (Barber et al., 2009). Additional concerns related to whether the 1983 Act was compatible with the Human Rights Act 1998, and this created another critical incentive for the full review of the legal framework.

In 1998 an Expert Committee was established to review the system and make recommendations. Its final report (DoH Expert Committee, 1999) set out a framework based on equality and self-determination and which considered individual capacity, all reflective of the wider mental health service and social care context. However, the subsequent Green Paper (DoH, 1999b) and White Paper (DoH, 2001) did not accept all of the recommendations and introduced additional restrictions for those considered to be suffering from dangerous and severe personality disorder. It appeared that the government response to the pressures for reform concentrated on how to address the gap between the criminal justice and mental health systems, and this was not well received by the mental health community. The resulting draft Bill was published in 2002 to significant opposition, with the Chairman of the Mental Health Alliance stating:

> . . . the government has chosen to link much-needed mental health law reform with issues of dangerousness and public protection, risking labelling everyone with a mental health problem in the public mind as potentially bad and dangerous. That is not acceptable. Violence is not a symptom of mental illness. Tragic, but isolated, cases are writ large in the public consciousness because of lurid and repeated media coverage.

(Mental Health Alliance, 2002)

The Bill was largely considered to be draconian and to strip away the rights of individuals rather than improving and modernising the system, and 50 organisations, including the General Medical Council, Royal College of Psychiatrists, MIND and the British Association of Social Work, openly condemned the proposals (Kmietowicz, 2002; MIND, 2003; Barber et al., 2009; Mental Health Alliance, 2002; 2003a; 2003b). The Mental Health Alliance, a coalition of 75 mental health-related organisations, was created to coordinate the many views, and in September 2002 a protest march took place, highlighting concerns about the Bill's powers and in particular community treatment orders.

Such cooperation between so many stakeholders was a landmark in the development of mental health law, and represented both the shift in attitudes towards mental health and the power of unity between professionals, organisations and service users. Although concern about draconian powers did not diminish, the government was also under continued pressure to address the gaps in services for those with personality disorder who might be at risk of committing violence. The balance between public protection and the rights and self-determination of individuals was irreconcilable in the provisions of the draft Bill, and as a result a stalemate between government and stakeholders was reached. In addition, the Joint Committee on Human Rights (2002) raised 13 points of concern in relation to the Bill's possible infringements.

The overwhelming negative response to the 2002 consultation resulted in the publication of a further Bill in 2004. This was also opposed, and a review by the Joint Parliamentary Committee on the Draft Mental Health Bill (2005) considered it to be lacking in clarity. In the background to these debates, the 'Bournewood' case was continuing through the court system and the Mental Capacity Act 2005 was given Royal Assent.

In 2006 the government announced that a new approach would be taken, and this time a smaller range of proposals were set out to introduce community treatment orders and amend and simplify the 1983 Act (DoH, 2006a). Reactions to these new proposals continued to be largely negative, and a statement from the British Medical Association (BMA) regarding both previous Bills said that the key issue was an ethical one that was yet to be addressed:

The central ethical concern about both draft Bills has been the lack of any requirement that compulsion should be allied to therapeutic benefit. Ethically the removal of fundamental rights must be justified by the reciprocal provision of health benefit, or it ceases to be health legislation and becomes a tool for maintaining social order.

(BMA, 2006; p.5)

Table 3.1 Key amendments to the Mental Health Act 1983

In addition to the deprivation of liberty provisions, there were nine key changes in the Mental Health Act 2007:

- **Definition of mental disorder** – simplified from four categories into a single definition: *'any disorder or disability of the mind'*.

- **Criteria for detention** – appropriate medical treatment introduced as a requirement of compulsion. Additionally, promiscuity, immoral conduct and sexual deviancy removed as explicit exclusion, as it was considered self-evident these were not mental disorder, despite some issues having diagnostic criteria in both DSM-IV and ICD-10 classifications.

- **Age-appropriate services** – recognition that children have been inappropriately detained and treated in adult wards and have specific needs that must be met. Consent and informal admission for under-18s also clarified.

- **Professional roles** – the role of approved social worker (ASW) replaced by approved mental health professional (AMHP) and the responsible medical officer (RMO) being replaced by the responsible clinician (RC), both of which include a wider range of professional groups in response to increasing multidisciplinary service arrangements. This met with some debate from all professions regarding the independence and grounding in the social model of mental health required to counterbalance the medical viewpoint.

- **Nearest relative** – civil partners given the same status as heterosexual married couples, an extension to displacement grounds to include 'unsuitability', and service users able to displace their own nearest relative.

- **Right to advocacy** – introduction of an advocacy role, the independent mental health advocate (IMHA), to whom all service users under compulsion would have access.

- **ECT and consent** – changes to capacity rules in relation to ECT, a patient with capacity, a valid advanced decision or a deputy who withholds consent, cannot be given ECT under the Mental Health Act against their wishes.

- **Supervised community treatment** – the most controversial of the amendments, supervised discharge, was abolished and a community treatment order (CTO) introduced. The CTO had the same criteria as a section 3 for treatment but could be applied to enforce compliance with treatment plans in the community, and included the ability to place conditions on individuals.

- **Referrals to MHRTs** – to support the aim of strengthening protection for service users, earlier and automatic referrals for tribunal reviews were introduced.

After a number of oppositions and amendments a significantly different piece of legislation from that proposed 8 years previously was finally passed and the Mental Health Act 2007 received Royal Assent in July 2007. By this time the 'Bournewood' case had also reached a resolution, and the amendments to the Mental Capacity Act 2005, relating to the Deprivation of Liberty Safeguards, were incorporated into the Mental Health Act 2007 to ensure that the gaps in the legislative framework were all addressed and that mental capacity and mental disorder were explicitly linked.

REFLECTION POINT

- *What is the impact of these changes from the perspective of social values?*

Comment

The amended legislation was a significant retreat by government, and although the CTO was introduced, the protections and powers available were not dramatically different from those of its predecessor. Some key factors to note are the amendments to the definition, which now encompasses personality disorders, the removal of exclusions relating to sexual behaviour, and the recognition of civil partnerships. These represent some significant advances in social thinking: in previous years sexual deviance was treated as a mental disorder and diagnostic categorisation occurred; despite this, these behaviours are no longer considered a mental health issue but rather a social, behavioural and value-based one, so embedded within the community consciousness that they no longer require explicit exclusion from mental health legislation.

The codes of practice as an ethical framework

One of the developments of the Mental Health Act 2007 was to explicitly enshrine the requirements to follow the Code of Practice (DoH, 2008a), a position that is also reflected in the Mental Capacity (DCA, 2007) and Deprivation of Liberty (DCA, 2008) legislation. The Code of Practice is the value base from which practitioners interpret and apply the law, and provides a range of direction and guidance to ensure ethical decision making.

The guiding principles set out in each Code of Practice (DoH, 2008a; DCA, 2007; 2008) are explicit value statements relating to how individuals with mental health issues should be treated. The emphasis on respect, participation and person-centred care is representative of the social welfare view that dominates current social policy and legislation. Although at times there is conflicting emphasis on public protection, in the main the mental health framework promotes safeguarding, involvement and participation of the individual and their social support system, and is consistent with current ethical thinking.

Table 3.2 The guiding principles of mental health legislation

Mental Health Act 2007	Mental Capacity Act 2005 (principles also cover DOLS)
Purpose Principle – ensuring that the use of restrictions or compulsion has a clear, explicit and appropriate purpose.	A person must be assumed to have capacity unless it is established that they do not. A person is not to be treated as unable to make a decision unless all practicable steps to help them do so have been taken without success.
Least restrictive principle – use of the minimum restriction necessary to ensure health and safety, or the safety of users.	
Respect principle – respect for patients' past and present wishes and diversity of situations and needs.	A person is not to be treated as unable to make a decision merely because they make an unwise decision.
Participation principle – involvement of patients (and carers) in their care and treatment.	An act done, or decision made, under this Act for or on behalf of a person who lacks capacity must be done, or made, in their best interests.
Effectiveness, efficiency and equity principle – treatment is effective, resources are used efficiently, and there is an equitable distribution of and access to services.	Before the act is done, or the decision is made, regard must be had to whether the purpose for which it is needed can be as effectively achieved in a way that is less restrictive of the person's rights and freedom of action.

The principles of both Acts are explicit value statements, and practitioners need to be aware of how they relate to their own professional value base. The continued drive towards service user choice and control is reflected in these codes. Empowerment, involvement and respect for diversity are core practice competencies for any mental health professional; however, for those undertaking a statutory role this can be difficult to balance when liberty and use of compulsory powers are being considered. Practitioners need to remember that although the individual may have little choice in terms of the application of compulsion, the means by which this is achieved and the subsequent treatment planning and risk management processes should be as participative as the individual will allow.

Ethics and mental health law

In historical terms mental health law (and other social legislation, such as the Poor Laws) were consistent with teleological ethics. The end justified the means, and although mental health issues were perceived socially as moral conditions, it was ethically acceptable to segregate the mentally ill from general society for the protection of both.

As treatment and understanding of mental health conditions developed, so did the ethics of psychiatric intervention, and whereas teleology remained the dominant school of thought, there was more consideration of the individual as a person, rather than a problem. The development of social welfare, and more humanistic approaches to those who were considered vulnerable, was reinforced by the establishment of the civil rights and user movements.

Today's mental health and mental capacity legislation has both teleological and deontological elements. Although a paternalistic theme persists that emphasises protection of the individual and a degree of control which is teleological in nature, the strengthening of service user rights and increased levels of involvement make the distinction that in some situations the means cannot be justified by the end, and an individual's rights are sacrosanct, a view that belongs to the school of deontological ethics. As already noted, the CTO was one of the controversial elements of the amended mental health legislation, and this was largely based on an ethical debate concerning whether placing conditions and controls on an individual in a community setting was acceptable.

Equalities and mental health law

One final area that must be considered is that of equality in the application of the legal framework. It has long been identified that certain groups are over-represented within the compulsive treatment system, and although the legislation and Codes of Practice are intended to be anti-discriminatory, the application is subject to human interpretation and presumption.

Practitioners in the statutory mental health system receive a range of training and supervision, all designed to enable reflection on decision making and address preconceptions and prejudices; however, statistically, the use of formal powers with groups such as black and ethnic minority (BME) populations remains over-represented (MHAC, 2003; 2005; 2009a; DoH, 2005a). Cultural competence and anti-oppressive practice will be considered in depth in Chapter 5, but it should be noted that practitioners must be aware of the equality issues that exist in relation to the use of formal powers. An awareness of how cultural beliefs, behaviours and norms can affect both an individual's mental well-being and their presentation to services is a basic competence that mental health professionals must develop.

REFLECTION POINT

- *What are the prejudices, stigmas or beliefs that could contribute to the over-representation of certain groups in compulsory mental health treatment?*

Comment

Mental health practitioners are subject to the pervading social values and beliefs, and issues such as stigma and stereotypes will have an impact on practice. The competence of workers in this context is to identify those values and beliefs and continually challenge themselves in terms of the rationale for decisions and ensuring that interventions are evidence-based and in the best interests of the individual.

Conclusion

This chapter has considered the origins and development of mental health law, and how the social context and values have affected them. The 20th century saw a range of landmark laws that have dramatically reformed the treatment system. Both the understanding of the causes and symptomology of mental health problems and the effectiveness of treatment have advanced significantly, and it is no longer considered ethical to segregate individuals or subject them to harsh treatments.

The current mental health legislative framework consists mainly of the Mental Health Act 2007 (amendment to the Mental Health Act 1983) and the Mental Capacity Act 2005. Both of these emphasise a value-based approach, with participation and empowerment being key.

In terms of the ethical debate there has been a shift towards a humanistic approach, and although protective measures are still considered necessary, the participation of the individual is an important element of any legal application of compulsive treatments.

Although anti-discrimination is embedded within the legal framework there remain equality concerns, and the social perception of certain groups can serve to compound their representation, BME and deaf populations being two of the key groups identified. Misconceptions about needs, cultures and behaviours can all contribute to this position, and practitioners need to remain aware of the potential issues and open to challenge where diversity could potentially affect a decision to apply compulsion.

Chapter summary

- Mental health law has developed alongside other social welfare legislation, with Poor Laws and the social welfare reforms of the 19th and 20th centuries having a significant impact on the treatment of individuals with mental health problems.

- Early treatment of people with mental health issues who were unable to support themselves was based on social attitudes that saw mental illness as a moral issue.

- The ethical dimension of mental health law has changed over time. Historically, segregation and containment were considered ethical, consistent with the view that society needed protection. As understandings have changed so have treatment approaches, and segregation and harsh treatments which were once commonplace are now unethical and in some cases inhumane.

- The person's rights have become a central consideration in contemporary legislation; however, this is a development of the 20th century and was historically not significant.

- Changes to the Mental Health Act 1983 received an unprecedented reaction from stake-holders, which included protest marches and a coalition being formed to represent the opposing views. This outcry represented a huge shift in the social value placed on treating those who have mental health issues, and should not be underestimated from a value-based perspective.

- The Codes of Practice for the Acts are essentially value statements, and practitioners are required to follow the directions that emphasise rights and safeguards for the individual.

- Over-representation of certain groups in the mental health system suggests that inequalities are still evident. Practitioners need to reflect on and understand the impact of diversity issues on their decisions and actions, and take action to challenge discrimination whenever it is encountered.

FURTHER READING

Bartlett, P (1999) *The Poor Law of Lunacy.* Leicester: Leicester University Press. Provides a comprehensive overview of the Poor Laws and early mental health legislation.

Barber, P, Brown, R and Martin, D (2009) *Mental Health Law in England and Wales.* Exeter: Learning Matters. Ideal for a comprehensive overview of contemporary legislation.

Brown, R (2009) *The Approved Mental Health Professional's Guide to Mental Health Law,* 2nd edition. Exeter: Learning Matters.

Chapter 4

Values in approved practice: empowerment and enforcement

CHAPTER OBJECTIVES

This chapter will assist readers in meeting the following mental health national occupational standards as relevant to all professional groups, including the statutory roles of AMHP and BIA under mental health and mental capacity legislation.

- A1 Develop your own knowledge and practice.

- J1 Work with people to identify their needs for safety, support and engagement, and how these needs can best be addressed.

- L6 Enable the views of groups, communities and organisations to be heard through advocating on their behalf.

Washing one's hands of the conflict between the powerful and the powerless means to side with the powerful, not to be neutral.

Paulo Freire, (1921–1997), Brazilian educator and
critical pedagogy theorist

Introduction

Working in mental health care often requires the practitioner to balance a range of conflicting demands. This is particularly evident in statutory roles such as approved mental health professional (AMHP) and best interest assessor (BIA); however, in mental health practice as a whole, power and empowerment should be seen as key.

There has always been an examination of power relationships in social work training, enshrined in the previous approved social worker (ASW) role and the dominance of the social model within the profession. However, for other colleagues the issues of power and its associated value base may be somewhat newer and hence more of a professional challenge.

The ethical considerations of both power and empowerment are complex, and the practitioner should carefully examine individual motives and use of skills, such as language and behaviour, to ensure that power relationships are acknowledged and transparent.

Empowerment is a subject that has received a great deal of attention over the past 20 years as a result of the increase in the voice of the service user movement and the prominence that government has given to choice, control and involvement in both legislation and guidance. There is now a significant evidence base demonstrating that empowerment can mean different things in different contexts; however, there is a common theme which shows that where there is choice and user control, outcomes are better for individual users and the effectiveness of services is increased.

It has been noted by a number of commentators (Masterson and Owen, 2006; Hui and Stickley, 2007; Foucault, 1982; Cleary, 2003) that in order to understand empowerment there must first be an understanding of what is meant by power.

This chapter will set out some of the key theories in relation to power, and then move on to consider empowerment, risk, and the issues associated with professional roles, including the availability of legal sanctions. The overall aim is to assist the practitioner to consider the wider ethical and value-based decisions involved in balancing the dual roles of enforcement and empowerment.

Theories of power

As with the ethical debates discussed in Chapter 3, the discipline of philosophy has a great deal to offer in terms of understanding what is meant by power, and how it is applied and exercised in health and social care. Psychiatry as a medical specialty has throughout its development considered power relationships; however, the transparent application of power, and the sharing of power between worker and service user, is rooted more comfortably within social models of disability.

A number of theorists have had a particular influence on the way we consider power in the context of sociology and psychology; a number of those ideas are set out here in order to provide the reader with an insight into how the construction of power has developed.

One of the key sociological theorists was Max Weber, a German social scientist, who wrote extensively on the issues of class, power and social stratification. In his 1947 work he defined power as:

> . . . *(a) the probability that (b) someone in a social relationship (c) will be able to achieve his or her will . . . (d) despite resistance and (e) regardless of the basis on which this probability rests.*

(Cited in Uphoff, 2004, p.221)

According to this analysis the assertion of power is not a certainty, but is rather based on probability; this is not a concrete thing, but rather the product of a relationship in which one party is able to influence another. The definition of whether power has been asserted is based on whether the individual has achieved the object they desired. In psychiatric terms this becomes less personalised, and is instead based on the professional aim of ensuring that the individual complies with the professional approach – for example whether they engage with the treatment plan, or show a reduction in problematic symptoms as a result.

Foucault, a French philosopher and sociologist, developed his view of the concept of power directly into the field of psychiatry; his theory was that humans are made 'subject to' others by means of both control and the creation of dependence (Foucault, 1982). This process has a direct influence upon the individual's sense of identity, and as such compounds the power relationship by creating a social norm and expectation. In the case of psychiatry, the individual begins to see themself as a 'psychiatry patient' as a core part of their identity. Although there may remain a degree of resistance to the treatment they are subjected to, there is also an expectation that the professional–patient relationship will have a unequal balance of power in favour of the professional. As a result, a degree of dependence is experienced, and a sense of powerlessness as the professional culture dominates the relationship.

The work of Bourdieu, a French sociologist, attempted to specify, in theoretical terms, the social restraints, power and orders that are produced as a result of indirect cultural mechanisms (Jenkins, 1992). This develops the concepts envisaged by Foucault, and suggests that whereas formal measures are available to mental health professionals, these are a small part of the whole in terms of the power relationship. Cultural and social understandings, which delegate authority to the professional and view the patient as in need of control, are far more significant in terms of the balance of power that exists within the field.

The final commentator considered here is Lukes, an American political and social theorist who defined what he termed as the 'three faces of power' (Lukes, 2005). This theory claims that there are three ways in which control of people can be exercised: decision-making, non-decision-making and ideological. Although the basis of the theory was constructed in relation to government action, the principles can be applied in the psychiatric setting.

Decision-making power is the most public of the three faces, and Lukes defines this as the power of governments to make policy decisions after consultation with opposition parties and the public. In mental health care this can be applied to such areas as Mental Health Act assessments: an AMHP will undertake an assessment, consult with others, including the subject of the assessment, and then make a decision which may affect the liberty of that individual.

Non-decision-making power is the power that governments have to control the agenda in debates and make certain issues unacceptable for discussion in moderate public forums. In mental health care this could include professional perspectives expressed about the efficacy of treatment models, which then influence the position and strategic direction of service developments. The issue of whether treatments such as psychosurgery and ECT are ethical, discussed in Chapter 3, is an example of this.

Ideological power is defined as the power to influence people's wishes and thoughts and make them want things that will not benefit them. This type of power can have a significant effect in the sociological and psychological context: an individual's understanding of self is a key example. Self-identification as a psychiatric patient, for example, can be construed as ideological power in action. This identification is a social construction – professional labels affecting the identity of the individual in a manner that can have far-reaching implications; this type of power links directly into theories such as social identity (Tajfel and Turner, 1986), discussed in Chapter 1. On an objective basis the individual would not necessarily choose the identification of psychiatric patient (or the associated social consequences); however, the dominant ideology in psychiatry is professional led, and so the individual becomes assimilated into this understanding.

Lukes' work in this area made a direct connection between value assumptions and the allocation of power: he stated that power was by both definition and usage:

> . . . *inextricably tied to a given set of (probably unacknowledged) value-assumptions which predetermine the range of its empirical application.*

> (Lukes, 2005: p.30)

For practitioners in the field these constructs are important, as they can have profound implications for the individual in terms of how they see themselves, how the public perceives them, and their experience of treatment overall.

The emphasis on empowering service users over the last decade has created a more open dialogue between user and worker; however, the power dynamics remain in favour of the practitioner, and so a thorough understanding of the types of power and influence that may be in play is needed if power-sharing and meaningful partnerships are to be developed.

REFLECTION POINT

- *What is your personal definition of power?*
- *How does your professional value base influence your understanding of power and how it is exercised?*
- *What types of power have you observed within your professional practice?*

Comment

How the practitioner defines and understands power has a significant impact on the task of empowerment. Power is not just about overall control of life choices: it may be that softer outcomes, for example choosing how to interact with your environment, can have profound implications for the individual. The sharing of information and involvement in treatment options are often empowering actions, and the practitioner needs to consider the full range of power and empowerment interactions and look beyond their own value base to try and understand how the service user experiences such actions.

Power dynamics, organisations and society

Although the majority of this chapter will consider the power relationships between service users and professionals, there are many complex levels of power dynamics within professions, organisations and society as a whole that also need consideration. The structure of modern society serves to reinforce discrimination in many forms, with age, race, class and economic status all creating divisions between individuals and groups (Dalrymple and Burk, 1995; Thompson, 2006; Gilbert, 2003). These divisions occur at both micro and macro levels, and can have a significant influence on the opportunities and experiences of the individual. At a micro level, for example within organisations, particular groups may be seen as more powerful than others. For example, doctors may have significantly more power and perceived social standing than other professions; or there may be divisions between qualified and unqualified staff that can result in unqualified staff having less of a voice in organisational decisions. On a macro level, for example between different cultures and social groups, there are differences in status, power and attitudes that may result in a particular group or individual being disadvantaged or marginalised.

These social structures and interactions are prevalent within both organisations and society as a whole, and can have significant impact on the individual and the extent to which their views are heard. Progress towards the full implementation of a social approach in mental health provision is one area that reflects these complex dynamics. Although social policy is emphasising the need for social context and inclusion to be core to mental health treatment, this has been hindered by both attitudes and power dynamics within professions and organisations.

The status society places on medical professionals is high, with sometimes unquestioning acceptance that 'Doctor knows best'. Although this has changed over recent years, with greater transparency and scrutiny, the perceived dominance of medical colleagues in mental health services is a product of the wider social perception, and is further perpetuated by a sense of powerlessness in social care practitioners who have found themselves operating in the unfamiliar cultural environment of the health service. Although there is an increasing shift towards an inclusive and integrated multidisciplinary provision, the extent to which this has been achieved is dependent upon local micro-systems and the prevailing power dynamics in each area.

A model of understanding discrimination and oppressive practices

Anti-discriminatory and anti-oppressive practices have for many years been a significant focus in critical social work and policy. One of the most significant models was that outlined by Neil Thompson (1993; 2006), who identified three levels of oppression – personal, cultural and structural (PCS).

This model links personal experience, beliefs and attitudes with the wider social group, and places it in the overall context of society, in order to understand and analyse discrimination and oppression, and the interactions between the individual and different social contexts. In order to apply anti-discriminatory practice within the mental health setting the practitioner needs to consider how these three levels interact, what is the resulting impact upon both the individual and their immediate social system, and how to challenge and influence these to improve the outcomes and experience of those affected.

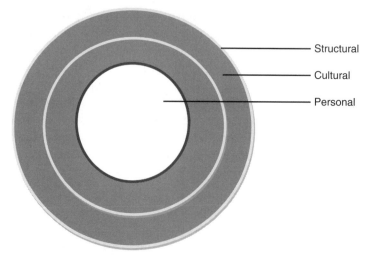

Figure 4.1 Thompson's PCS Model
(Source: Thompson, 1993, 2006)

Personal (P) level

This is concerned with an individual's attitudes, particularly in relation to prejudice against a certain group of people, for example racism or homophobia. It is located in the middle, because individual beliefs and ideas are supported through two other levels.

Cultural (C) level

This relates to the 'shared values' or 'commonalities' within groups and communities, for example beliefs about what is right and wrong, good or bad.

Structural (S) level

This relates to how divisions and oppression are a fundamental part of society, supported through institutions such as the media, religion and politics that support both cultural norms and personal beliefs and serve to cement these beliefs into society.

Defining empowerment

The term empowerment is commonly used in both health and social care from both a policy and a practice point of view. This is a complex concept within mental health provision, as aspects such as legal sanctions, social construction of risk and fluctuation of the individual's capacity are all issues the practitioner must grapple with to ensure that both the individual and the public are safeguarded.

Empowerment appears to have a range of meanings, with no common agreed definition. It has been said that it is often easier to define empowerment by its absence (Rappaport, 1984), as the concept can take different forms for different people within different contexts, and indeed the application of a single definition could result in a formulaic or prescriptive approach, which would itself be contradictory (Zimmerman, 1984). Despite these differences, a number of key themes are evident in the literature that can be directly applied to mental health.

Rather than a specific definition, the term is often applied in terms of moving away from being disempowered or a passive recipient of care, and being able to exercise personal power or control in one's social context (Maclean, 1995; Segal, 1995). This has also been termed as an individual having choice and control.

Attributes of empowerment that have been cited include:

- having decision-making power over own situation;
- having access to a range of options;
- having a voice;
- having, and exercising, individual rights.

> (Rogers et al., 1997; Rappaport, 1990; Dalrymple and Burke, 1995;
> Thompson, 1993)

These themes appear to be common across the disciplines, and so the definition to be applied in this text is:

> *The process by which the individual can make choices, express their own views and preferences, influence their own situations, and take control and responsibility for their own actions.*

The idea of responsibility must go hand in hand with the idea of choice and control, if mental health service users are to be truly empowered; personal responsibility should be an integral part of the construction, no action is consequence free, and to be empowered we must also be accountable.

This definition and the associated implications have a number of effects in the context of mental health care. The mental health system has historically taken away individual responsibility, with professional decision making taking precedence over self-determination because of the perceptions of capability and risk that have been applied to individuals experiencing mental distress. This is a key area where value-based assumptions and ethical considerations must be examined.

Societal views of what mental illness means to the individual are many, and practitioners are as susceptible to these views as anyone. Whereas working with those experiencing mental distress will go some way to breaking down misinformed belief systems, there remains a range of preconceived beliefs. The lack of uptake of direct payments in mental health serves as an example, as practitioners are the route of access for users of a range of services, and if the practitioner has doubts about the application of a particular option, the service user will either have reduced access to such possibilities, or even find that doubt transferred to them and hence be less likely to engage in that option.

The aim of empowering service users to take control of their own situations is often affected by such anxieties, and although professional groups espouse the value of self-determination, many factors can prevent its full realisation. The concept of risk is a key factor here, societal views of mental health service users being intertwined with the potential and actual risks posed by and to individuals, and the next section will consider risk within a power and empowerment context and ask 'how does risk affect the power dynamics between service user and professional?'

- *What types of activities have you carried out, or observed, in your practice area that could be considered as empowering service users or carers?*

Comment

Power and empowerment are about small as well as large choices, and the practitioner needs to be aware of the impact of day-to-day options on the service user's experience.

The concept of risk

The general conception of the risks posed by individuals with mental health problems are rooted in historical understandings, social misconceptions of dangerousness, media presentations (Pulzer, 2008; Shift, 2006, 2008) and reactions to incidents of violence, aggression and suicide (Szmukler, 2000; Petch, 2001). All of these elements have a range of complexities and social meanings that compound a system of care that has been focused largely on professionally led risk aversion (Morgan, 2007a).

The concept of risk is difficult to define: it is embedded in sociology and psychology, and has received a great deal of attention as many commentators have attempted to develop a definition that encompasses the complexities of social interpretation and the changing expectations and norms created by social and technological advances (Kahneman and Tversky 2000; Gigerenzer, 2003; Beck 1992; Douglas 1994; Foucault 1991; Lupton 2000). Although there are many views on what constitutes risk, two key commonalities must be acknowledged:

- Risk may be mitigated but not eliminated; risk in its basic form refers to the uncertainty of outcome from any given action – this may be positive or negative.

- Social context influences how risk is perceived and what risks are deemed acceptable within a given culture.

Within the mental health system the unpredictability of behaviour and symptoms is a particular concern, combined with the view that those with mental health problems may not be able to act rationally or be competent to make decisions (Alaszewski, 2002; Langan, 1999). For the public this fear is based on misconceptions, and for professionals is rooted in a blame culture that looks to them when things go wrong (Vize, 2007; Santry, 2007; Stanley and Manthorpe, 2004). As a result, the professional cultures veer towards paternalism, protectionism, and an unwillingness to enable those seen as vulnerable to take risks that might have negative consequences.

Dealing with negative consequences, including personal failure, is a facet of the human condition and is often the way people learn; to prevent it is to prevent individual growth.

This has been recognised by both government and professional groups over the last decade, and as a result the term 'positive risk' is becoming more evident. This does not mean that risk-averse practice has been relegated to history, but in some areas positive risk, and outcomes such as increased choice and control, are gaining popular support, and this fits firmly into the empowerment agenda in mental health care.

ACTIVITY 4.1

Consider some of your daily activities that could have a risk or uncertain outcome attached. Make a list of them (some examples are smoking, driving a car, crossing the road) and consider the following:

- *Why do you take the risks you have listed?*
- *What is society's view of the activities you have listed?*
- *Are there any cultures you can think of that would not take the risks you have listed?*

Everyone takes risks every day; the level of risk that is acceptable to the person varies according to context, beliefs and cultural norms. The individual's context and experience act as a filter to assist in deciding which risks are acceptable and which are not.

Positive risk

Positive, or supported, risk taking has received significant attention in mental health since 2000. The idea has been largely developed from the work of Morgan (2000, 2004, 2007b), who defined it as:

> *Weighing up the potential benefits and harms of exercising one choice of action over another. Developing plans and actions that reflect the positive potentials and stated priorities of the service user. Using available resources and support to achieve the desired outcomes, and to minimise the potential harmful outcomes.*

(Morgan, 2007a; p. 37)

This concept is built upon the way each of us makes decisions about the risks we will or will not take, and takes the process into the care environment by placing it within a framework that the practitioner and service user can define and explore together. It is seen as the means by which service users can be empowered to control their own actions, decisions and situations, and is being heavily promoted within the mental health system (DoH, 2007d; 2007e). Practitioners are now required to balance risk decisions to ensure that service users are both enabled and protected, a task that can be very difficult to manage.

Those with mental health difficulties are no different from anyone else, and whereas the stigma campaigns, user movements and user–worker alliances have made great strides towards embedding choice and self-determination within the care system, the operation of risk assessment and management appears to have lagged behind, and in terms of values and ethics this is problematic.

The current framework of ethics and values in mental health is focused on participation and involvement – indeed, the core competency requirements of all the professions now includes aspects such as engagement and empowerment. The personalisation agenda continues to promote these aims and ideas, and in this climate risk aversion could be described as unethical, as it potentially restricts the rights and responsibilities of the individual in a manner that is unacceptable to cultural and social norms. There is, however, a paradox here, for although mental health service users must have choice and control over their lives, they must also be controlled and restrained where there may be a risk to others. Practitioners are both therapeutic allies and agents of the state, and this can be a difficult balance to achieve. Whereas social work and psychiatry have both long since recognised these competing demands, other professional groups may find this more difficult to apply, as they have previously been able to hand such decisions over to others.

Risk, empowerment and enforcement: a mental health phenomenon

The expanded role of the approved mental health professional (AMHP) and the new role of best interest assessor (BIA) under the Mental Capacity Act 2005 represent a significant change, and the power dynamic created by undertaking these roles should not be underestimated.

The value base attached to such duties is intrinsic to the training and supervision that is required, and the competency framework relates to identifying and addressing imbalances by ensuring that they are transparent, the least restrictive alternative possible, proportionate to the presenting risks, and appropriate in the circumstances.

These elements help to ensure that the decision to exercise power over another is not taken lightly; however, the ability of the professional to apply such measures, whether or not they do so, is the element that skews the balance in the first instance, and serves to reinforce the view that professional decisions take precedence over user's wishes. In mental health this is common: aspects such as concordance, engagement and insight are all considered in risk assessment processes. The right of the individual to choose not to take medication because of unpleasant side effects, for example, may be overridden by the risk of relapse that results from exercising this choice. This is not the case with other service user groups, for example cardiac patients; the following case study considers this issue.

CASE STUDY *4.1*

Simon is a 42-year-old man who is diagnosed with paranoid schizophrenia; he has a range of symptoms, including depression, thought disorder, deliberate self-harm, auditory hallucinations and delusional beliefs that others are trying to harm him. During phases of active illness he has been known to barricade himself in his flat and disconnect all electrical appliances. He has no history of violence or aggression towards others, and his self-harm consists of shallow cutting to his forearms and thighs; he has been admitted to hospital on one occasion during the last 5 years, and this was on a section 2 of the Mental Health Act 1983. He is prescribed several medications including clozapine, and complains of several side effects, including constipation, sedation and significant weight gain. He is very distressed about the weight gain. Simon tends to take his medication when unwell, and once he is feeling better stops taking them. Simon is assessed as having capacity in relation to his care at this time and is not currently concordant.

Steven is a 42-year-old man diagnosed with chronic heart disease; he has a range of symptoms, including shortness of breath, angina, apnoea and hypertension. He is over-weight and smokes 20+ cigarettes a day. He is prescribed a range of medications to control his symptoms, but takes them irregularly as he experiences a range of side effects, including stomach upset, constipation and headaches. His symptoms have fluctuated over the past 5 years; he has been admitted to general hospital twice for hypertension, and has experienced one heart attack during this time. Steven could improve his symptoms with exercise and diet, but has so far been unwilling to make the necessary lifestyle changes.

- *Which case poses the most risks? Why, and to whom?*

- *Are the decisions made by Steven and Simon rational? Why?*

- *What interventions would you make in each case? Why?*

- *What rights do Simon and Steven have in their situations? What are the differences?*

Both Simon and Steven are making choices that could be questioned; however, the mental health aspect of Simon's case means that power can be exercised to curb those choices: this is not based on his capacity, but rather the professional view of what is the best option. As a result it is possible to suggest that Simon's rights are less than those of Steven, regardless of the possible severe outcome in each case.

This is an ethical dilemma for the practitioner, as it is clear both service users are at times acting contrary to what could be considered in their own best interests, and as such is a clear example of the use of power.

Individual rights

One of the key roles that AMHPs and BIAs are required to undertake is to ensure that where deprivation or restrictions of liberty are applied the individual's rights are considered and safeguarded.

In the mental health system the issue of individual rights may at times be restricted: this is acknowledged in the European Convention on Human Rights (ECHR) and the Human Rights Act 1998, which allow for the lawful restriction of liberty of individuals considered to be of 'unsound mind' (Article 5, ECHR). The term is not defined in any concrete fashion, as it is a matter of professional judgement; however, it is stated that it is 'more than a deviation from normal societal views or behaviour', and that reference to relevant domestic law and the particular circumstances of the case in light of current psychiatric knowledge is required (Winterwerp v The Netherlands, 1979). The domestic definition applied in the UK was amended by the Mental Health Act 2007, and is now 'any disorder or disability of the mind' (s1).

This legal framework allows for the restriction of an individual's liberty and the application of coercive treatment, but it does not remove other rights. The roles of both AMHPs and BIAs are concerned with ensuring that individual rights are observed. In some cases this may be ensuring that the individual's wishes are considered (as set out in the guiding principles of both the Mental Health Act and the Mental Capacity Act Codes of Practice (DoH, 2008a; DCA, 2007), and in all cases it involves ensuring that the individual is aware of their rights to appeal, the rights of their representative (nearest relative in the case of the MHA), the right to review by a tribunal and the right to representation by an advocate (legal and/or independent). These safeguards are in place to ensure that restrictions are not applied unduly, and to continually monitor the decisions made by professionals in terms of proportionality and appropriateness.

In the context of risk and power, it can still be suggested that although the individual retains rights, these do not represent a real shift in power. The clinical judgement of professionals remains a core element in the decision making of independent reviewers, and the same cultural and social factors remain in evidence. This is not to suggest that detention and compulsion are not required – on the contrary; in many cases compulsive treatment is the most appropriate option in light of the risks associated with an individual's condition; however, the aim of this discussion is to highlight the issue of power dynamics, and to identify that although individuals have rights, these can be, and often are, overridden. Practitioners therefore need to remain critical of the basis of their decision making, including considering possible beliefs, assumptions, prejudices and value judgements.

Empowerment, enforcement and ethics

This chapter has considered a range of issues, starting with theories of power and empowerment, and moving on to the role of risks and rights in the application of both. It is clear that there is a range of complexities that practitioners must navigate in the user–worker relationship, and the availability of legal sanctions creates a dynamic that is always present in these relationships.

Although the AMHP and BIA roles are entrenched in the power dynamics, the role of all mental health practitioners is influenced by this differential. This means that the core values and consideration of the ethical application of power is necessary at all times. The focus on empowerment of users is a welcome development in mental health care; however, this is not a straightforward task: social views and professional judgements are not always objective, and need to be deconstructed to enable the practitioner to develop a reflective and ethical approach to both empowerment and enforcement.

Presumptions about risk and capacity also have a role to play: although protection of those who may be vulnerable is a core part of the professional role, the need to move beyond the legacy of paternalistic care and to recognise that risk is a part of everyday life is also clear. Mental distress does not mean that an individual is unable to make decisions or take responsibility for their own actions, and assuming this is the case is a fundamental flaw. In order for empowerment to be meaningful the individual needs to experience both rights and responsibility, and this combination can add to the experience of recovery and the achievement of fuller social inclusion.

With regard to the role of ethics, the professional needs to ensure that their actions are undertaken in an appropriate, proportionate and informed manner. The ability to exercise coercion should never be downplayed: the aim of a transparent application of power requires the worker to identify the power dynamics and to ensure that the individual's rights are observed at all times. Coercion is neither a threat nor an incentive: it should only be used if it becomes necessary according to the criteria set down in law, and disagreement between worker and user is never sufficient justification.

The ability to balance the dual roles of empowerment and enforcement can be very difficult to manage: it is a paradox that professionals are required to reconcile within themselves. Reflective and critical examination of their own practice remains essential throughout the professional's career to ensure that the power relationship is acknowledged and managed, and that practice is at all times ethical. Understanding the theoretical basis for the aspects of practice discussed in this chapter can help the practitioner develop and maintain their competence and to translate theory into the practice environment. The skill of a practitioner is to recognise that both elements of the balance are developed in a context of individual, community and wider society, as only in this way can competence be achieved.

Chapter summary

- Concepts of power and empowerment need to be understood in context, and applied to inform the practice environment and support a values-based approach.

- The understanding of power can be used to inform practice. Is it ethical to exercise power for protection purposes? Teleological thought would suggest that this is the case, and the Mental Health Act supports this view; however, in the case of psychological health or other decision making the individual has the right to make poor choices, and this cannot be eroded in the same way as for those experiencing mental health difficulties. This situation is largely based on symptoms, diagnosis and behaviour, rather than rationality and capacity, and the practitioner needs to remain aware of these dynamics and the areas that influence them, such as legal frameworks, social values and cultural norms.

Masterson, S and Owen, S (2006) Mental health service users' social and individual empowerment: Using theories of power to elucidate far-reaching strategies. *Journal of Mental Health*, 15 (1), 19–34.

Morgan, S (2004) *Positive Risk-Taking: An Idea Whose Time Has Come.* Health Care Risk Report, October 2004, 18–19.

Thompson, N (2006) (4th Ed) *Anti-Discriminatory Practice.* Basingstoke: Palgrave Macmillan.

Chapter 5
Equality and diversity

Daisy Bogg and Harjinder Bahra

CHAPTER OBJECTIVES

This chapter will assist readers in meeting the following mental health national occupational standards as relevant to all professional groups, including the statutory roles of AMHP and BIA under mental health and mental capacity legislation.

- M4 Develop, maintain and evaluate systems and structures to promote the rights, responsibilities and diversity of people.

Human diversity makes tolerance more than a virtue; it makes it a requirement for survival.

René Jules Dubos (1901–1982) French-American microbiologist, experimental pathologist, environmentalist, humanist, and winner of the Pulitzer Prize

Introduction

The issue of equality and diversity has received a great deal of attention across health and social care services, and particularly with mental health. As a result of a range of inquiries, and also statistical evidence showing that black and minority ethnic (BME) groups are over-represented in the formal mental health system (DoH, 2005a; MHAC, 2005), the emphasis in services is on race rather than diversity, and this chapter seeks to explore all six strands of the equality and diversity framework (gender, age, race, religion, sexuality and disability) to help readers consider the varied needs of the population that experience mental health difficulties and may be in need of support.

It has been recognised that social context has a significant impact upon recovery from mental health problems, and as discussed in Chapter 3, stigma and prejudice have the potential to create barriers and have a negative influence on individual prognosis. As discussed in Chapter 4, roles such as the AMHP and BIA are particularly concerned with the power relationships between professionals and service users, and discrimination, whether direct or indirect, can contribute to this dynamic and disadvantage an individual.

Anti-discriminatory practice (ADP) is an element that must be applied to each role, although the terminology falls within the domain of social work. The value *challenge discriminatory images and practices affecting individuals, families, carers, groups and communities* (TOPSS UK, 2002) should not be social work-specific, but applied equally to the wider mental health practice context, including AMHP and BIA practice. The equality and diversity framework is explicitly linked to ADP, and all practitioners are required to develop a culturally competent practice that is sensitive to a range of needs.

As an starting point it is useful to understand what is meant by discrimination, and the different types of discrimination that can be experienced in our society. The next section will seek to identify these understandings and the impact they may have on an individual's experience and recovery journey, before moving on to discuss how ADP is applied, and then finally the possible needs and experiences of those whose needs are specific to the six strands of equality and diversity mentioned above.

Direct and indirect discrimination

The *Oxford Dictionary* definition of discrimination is:

> *the unjust or prejudicial treatment of different categories of people or things.*

> (Oxford English Dictionary, 2009)

Within the equality and diversity framework this is extended to include a range of areas, and within the mental health system there is a stigmatisation of mental illness itself that compounds any other differences that may be present. Discrimination can be direct – meaning that there is an explicit exclusion of the individual as a result of their difference; or indirect – meaning that a lack of awareness or adaptation to their difference is the cause of the exclusion.

Social stigma and prejudice are examples of discrimination, and mental health service users can often find that society and the community are unwilling to engage with them (Wahl, 1999; Schulze and Angermeyer, 2003; Dinos et al., 2004). This can be expressed directly in the form of explicit rejection, ridicule or aggression, or indirectly in the form of dismissal or avoidance. This is largely based on fear and misunderstanding of what mental illness means, and it is not uncommon for questions of capability and risk to be presented as reasons for exclusion.

Indirect discrimination is often more complex to identify, as it results from a lack of understanding and adaptation rather than a direct and explicit rejection or exclusion. With physical disability it is easier to define. Wheelchair access is a classic example: the inability to access certain premises or services because of a lack of ramps or insufficient space to accommodate a wheelchair would be an example of indirect discrimination.

For those with mental health issues, indirect discrimination is based more on attitudes and social norms and as such is not easy to identify. Some types of stigma and stereotyping can be defined as indirect discrimination: for example presuming that an individual is unable to make decisions or unable to take part in a cognitive activity; however, manifestations of this could be either direct, leading to direct exclusion, or indirect leading to inclusion but within a limited framework, for example needing consent from a carer or professional prior to taking part in an activity.

Discrimination in both forms can have a negative impact upon mental well-being: rejection and exclusion can have a detrimental effect on individuals without mental health difficulties, but for those who experience mental distress such discrimination affects their sense of self-worth and overall self-image (Corrigan and Watson, 2002; Corrigan, 2004; Angermeyer and Matschinger, 2004; Pinfold et al., 2005).

Equality, diversity and human rights

Equality, diversity and human rights are all terms used in social and health policy. It is useful to consider what they mean, as in order to practice in a competent manner, professionals in these areas need to be aware of the requirements and implications of each.

Equality is not about being politically correct, but about achieving social justice at home, at work, and in the community. Equality looks at how age, disability, gender, race, religion or belief and sexual orientation could be create barriers to social interaction, services, employment and training, and tries to address those issues (McPherson, 2008; Braveman and Gruskin, 2003; Riley, 2002).

Human rights are the rights and freedoms that belong to all of us all of the time. They cannot be 'taken away', but can be claimed, fulfilled or limited in certain circumstances. They regulate the relationship between public authorities and ordinary citizens by setting the basic standards below which authorities must not go. They also place a duty of care on public authorities to treat individuals and groups with fairness, respect, equality, dignity and autonomy – the FREDA principles (Joint Committee on Human Rights, 2008).

Human rights were first legally defined in the 1948 Universal Declaration of Human Rights in response to the Holocaust. They were adapted in Europe as the European Convention on Human Rights (to which the UK signed up in 1951). In 1998 the European Convention became enshrined in the Human Rights Act (UK), when it received Royal Assent, and it came into force in 2000. The Human Rights Act (UK) was a significant moment because it required that UK courts and all public authorities must comply with the European Convention when making any decision that would affect ordinary citizens.

Diversity is whatever makes us different from each other: it is not limited to culture, religion, race or ethnicity, but includes social status, financial status, education, class, gender, sexual orientation, age, disability and the many other differences that make an individual unique (Capitman, 2002; Sorofman, 1986). Moreover, diversity is not static. An individual's view on life and events may change with time, their environment and the choices they make. Sometimes the simple process of watching a movie, reading a book or an article can move us sufficiently to give a different dimension to previously held views.

In legal terms, diversity is broadly defined as the six equality strands of age, disability, gender, race, religion or belief and sexual orientation, but when we drill down the equality strands we may find prejudices, misunderstanding, fear and anxieties about the unknown.

REFLECTION POINT

Consider your own understanding of equality and diversity.

- *How does your approach change when dealing with individuals with different social or cultural contexts?*

Comment

The practitioner should be adaptable and flexible in the context of diverse understandings, experiences and needs – issues such as language, non-verbal communication, the types and formats of information provided, the types of support offered, consideration of the wider community, the involvement of others in the assessment and care planning processes, and the extent to which the wider system influences decisions are all important yet dynamic elements of an individual's understanding and experience.

The drive towards equality, diversity and human rights approaches in mental health services is embedded in legislation and policy. The government's commitment to ensure equity and choice can be seen throughout health and social care developments over the last decade, and the role of the mental health practitioner, whether generic or statutory, is to ensure that these principles are adhered to.

Policy and legislative drivers for the equality and diversity agenda

The equality and diversity agenda is clearly contained in the policy and legislative frameworks for health and social care, and the practitioner needs to be aware of the drivers for such aspects of practice, which are set out in this section.

The idea of fairness for all is at the heart of health and social care. It is also widely recognised that a 'one size fits all' approach is not always appropriate, particularly in a diverse society. Equality of outcomes and personalised services will only be delivered by working with the community, recognising difference and tailoring provision to meet differing needs (DoH, 2006b, 2009b, 2009c, 2009d; Cass et al., 2009). This system was born out of the ideal that care should be available to all, regardless of wealth. Equality and human rights legislation now covers almost every aspect of the delivery of this aim, and key Department of Health policies demonstrate how crucial it is for those who commission and provide services to do so by ensuring that people's individual needs, their dignity and their human rights are respected at every stage.

The NHS Constitution (DoH, 2009c) and the *Putting People First* (DoH, 2007c) guidance are two of these key policy documents. The NHS Constitution was published in 2009. Its first principle states:

> *The NHS provides a comprehensive service, available to all irrespective of gender, race, disability, age, sexual orientation, religion or belief. It has a duty to each and every individual that it serves and must respect their human rights. At the same time, it has a wider social duty to promote equality through the services it provides and to pay particular attention to groups or sections of society where improvements in health and life expectancy are not keeping pace with the rest of the population.*

(p.3)

This document requires that all NHS bodies and private and third-sector providers supplying NHS services will have regard to the Constitution in their decisions and actions, which include the principles of equality and diversity.

Putting People First was published in 2007 and set out a framework to support independent living for all adults. Personalised services that support independence and dignity will only be possible if we take account of people's different characteristics, heritage, traditions and beliefs, and real change will only be achieved through their participation at every stage. The health and social care system's ambitions for personalisation are therefore critical to the wider ambitions for equality and diversity.

In addition, two further significant strategic changes support the 'designing in' of equality and diversity at a local level. *High Quality Care for All* (Darzi, 2008), the final report of the NHS Next Stage Review, set out a vision to make quality the organising principle of the NHS, where quality is understood not only in terms of clinical and other outcomes but also in terms of the experiences of service users. The Department is clear that 'high-quality care for all' will not be realised without systematic attention to equality and human rights. For social care, the *Care and Support* Green Paper (DoH, 2009d) sets out a vision for a system that promotes choice and control, and ensures that everyone can receive the high-quality care and support they need – where support is targeted at those most in need. Again, the centrality of equality and human rights to this agenda is clear.

Equality, diversity and the workforce

For the NHS and social care providers to deliver the requirements of the national policy and strategy, staff must be committed to delivering high-quality care to all service users; equality and human rights must therefore be integral to workforce development. To support this, the government has published its workforce strategy as part of the NHS Next Stage Review, *A High Quality Workforce* (DoH, 2008b) and social care has followed suit with *Working to Put People First* (DoH, 2009e). Both of these documents set out strategies to support health and social care organisations develop and support a multidisciplinary skilled workforce that will help to bring about the improvements in equality and outcomes and is representative of the population served.

The role of regulation in the equality and diversity agenda

On 1 April 2009 a new regulatory body, the Care Quality Commission (CQC), came into being. This merged three previous authorities – the Health Care Commission (HCC), the Commission for Social Care Inspection (CSCI) and the Mental Health Act Commission (MHAC), which was a positive step for mental health as it supports the current integrated model of delivery and applies a single set of standards and a single inspection and regulation process. One of the key aspects the CQC is set to introduce is a provider registration process, which will require service providers to meet mandatory equality, diversity and human rights outcomes. Some of the key outcomes for registration that will support the delivery of the agenda within mental health care, include (CQC, 2009):

- **Safeguarding vulnerable people** People using the service are protected from abuse, or the risk of abuse, and their human rights are respected.

- **Ensuring personalised care** People who use services should receive care, treatment and support from all staff (including volunteers and ancillary staff) who are committed to maximising people's choice, control and social inclusion and upholding their rights as an important way of reducing the potential for abuse.

- **Suitability of staff** The staff who provide services should be appropriately trained, skilled and qualified in the area of diversity and human rights, ensuring that they are able to respond appropriately and are sufficiently aware of the issues that people face.

- **Promotion of rights and choices** People who use services are able to use the complaints and comments process and know they will be treated fairly and their concerns responded to in a way that respects their human rights and diversity.

- **Respecting and involving people who use services** Promoting and respecting their privacy and dignity by ensuring that staff treat people sensitively by understanding and respecting their diversity.

- **Consent to care and treatment – promotion of rights and choices** People are able to make a decision about whether or not to give consent because they have information in a way they can understand that takes into account their diversity, including information about alternatives, risks and benefits.

- **Meeting the needs of people** Providers should have knowledge and understanding of how equal opportunities and a respect for human rights and diversity are put into practice when delivering the service.

Although many of these areas have been explicit in professional Codes of Practice and organisational structures for some time, the statutory requirement for organisations to demonstrate these in order to operate increases the emphasis and the need for evidencing in the practice environment.

REFLECTION POINT

- *How do you evidence your consideration of the principles of equality and diversity within your role and practice?*

Comment

How an individual experiences and responds to care and support, and their understanding of their distress, is influenced by their life experiences and social context. The building of working relationships, the care planning and assessment processes and the opportunities that can be accessed to enhance recovery are all aspects that a practitioner should be able to evidence.

The legal context

Discrimination law is a very complex area: there are four key elements that the practitioner needs to be aware of. As well as direct and indirect discrimination, harassment and victimisation are also central, particularly from a safeguarding perspective.

The definitions of harassment and victimisation are as follows:

- **Harassment** – unwanted behaviour that is offensive, frightening or in any way distressing, including violation of a person's dignity, or creating an intimidating, hostile, degrading or offensive environment (includes bullying).

- **Victimisation** – treating someone less favourably because they have made or intend to make a complaint or allegation, or have given or intend to give evidence in relation to a complaint of discrimination.

The first set of equality legislation in England was passed in the 1970s, and covered discrimination on grounds of sex and race in the fields of employment, education, and the provision of goods, facilities and services. Since then, protection against discrimination has been extended to cover age (in relation to employment), disability, gender and transgender status, religion and belief and sexual orientation.

The Equality Bill, passed through Parliament during 2009, further strengthens the law by banning age discrimination in the provision and the discharge of public functions; and by creating a single new equality duty on public bodies covering age, disability, race, gender, religion or belief and sexual orientation.

The disability, gender and race equality duties

The Sex Discrimination Act 1975, the Race Relations Act 1976 and the Disability Discrimination Act 1995 prohibit discrimination on the grounds of gender, race and disability, respectively, in the fields of employment, education and the provision of goods, facilities and services. Public authorities are also subject to a positive duty to integrate equality considerations into their work and to consider taking positive steps to address disadvantage. The Race Relations Act 1976 was amended by the Race Relations (Amendment) Act 2000 to introduce a new section 71, which sets out a new duty in relation to racial equality. The purpose of this was to alter the focus of legislation from discrimination alone to also include a proactive requirement to attempt to prevent discrimination arising. The amendment imposed a duty on public authorities to have due regard to the need to eliminate unlawful racial discrimination, to promote equality of opportunity, and to promote good relations between different racial groups.

In 2005 and 2006, similar public sector duties were introduced in relation to disability and gender. All public authorities are bound by these statutory equality duties, set out in sections 76A and B of the Sex Discrimination Act 1975, section 71 of the Race Relations Act 1976, and sections 49A and D of the Disability Discrimination Act 2005. Secondary legislation made under those sections set out further specific duties.

> *RESEARCH SUMMARY*
>
> ### Inequality in mental health: the evidence
>
> *There is a great deal of evidence to suggest that inequalities exist for black and minority ethnic (BME) people in the field of mental health (Campbell and McLean, 2002; Keating et al., 2003; Singh et al., 2007; Dein et al., 2007; McGrath et al., 2004), including the incidence of mental health conditions, access to and experience of mental health services, and outcomes.*
>
> *Kirkbride et al.'s 2006 study on aetiology and ethnicity in schizophrenia and other psychoses found rates of psychosis in England up to nine times higher for African-Caribbean communities than for the white British population, and six times higher for African communities (and smaller increased risks for other BME groups). Other studies (Cantor-Graae and Selten, 2005; Bray et al., 2006; Livingston et al., 2001; Pernice and Brook, 1994) have found elevated rates of mental illness among migrant populations worldwide. Following on from these findings the 2008 Foresight Report on future challenges for mental health (Jenkins et al., 2008) summarises the evidence thus:*
>
> > Immigrants are at much greater risk of psychoses than native-born groups, the risk typically varying between 2–8 times higher in various immigrant populations. Elevated rates extend into the descendants of immigrants, so-called 'second generation' groups, too, suggesting migration and/or post-migratory environmental experiences are likely to be important in the aetiology of disorder. Factors to explain raised rates in immigrants and their descendants include: stressful life events, discrimination, urban living and socioeconomic deprivation, all of which are to some degree correlated.
>
> > (p. 39)
>
> *Since 2005 an annual census of BME patients in the mental health system has been conducted, called 'Count Me In'. The project was developed in conjunction with the former Healthcare Commission and former Mental Health Act Commission, and its purpose was to evaluate mental health and learning disability services from the perspective of BME people; to collect accurate information on a range of patient characteristics, including ethnicity, language and religion; and to help NHS and independent organisations that provide mental health and learning disability services ensure that services are culturally relevant and appropriate.*

Race and discrimination

Divisions between racial groups remain a significant social concern, with themes such as the higher likelihood of socioeconomic deprivation, lower levels of education, higher unemployment and increased contact with the criminal justice system than white counterparts all being highlighted. It is clear that inequalities in relation to race are also evident within mental health care, with the Mental Health Commission reports (MHAC, 2003, 2005, 2007, 2009a) continuing to highlight higher rates of detention for BME groups under section 136 of the Act. Since 2005 the Count Me In census has consistently found rates of admission for the black ethnic groups to be around three times higher than average; this disparity was also found in the 2009 North East Public Health Observatory report

(Glover and Evison, 2010), which demonstrates that such differences remain an issue in the current system.

Considering the issue of race equality within Thompson's PCS model, it is possible to suggest that individual and microsystem responses are a product of structural issues within our society. There is thus a need for greater emphasis on social deprivation and equality in order to effect improvements in the microsystem of mental health care.

CASE STUDY 5.1

Stuart and Simon are both patients on the local acute inpatient ward. Stuart is a 23-year-old white man from a working-class family. The family live on a local housing estate where there are significant racial tensions and gang activity. Simon is 33 and of African-Caribbean descent; his parents are second-generation immigrants, and Simon considers himself to be British.

Following a disturbance one lunchtime Stuart and Simon have an argument and Stuart shouts racist comments at Simon. The staff intervene to break up the argument. Simon feels that the racist remarks have not been dealt with. Stuart says he does not understand what the problem is and the argument is over, and the staff are unwilling to reopen the disagreement, as they feel the ward is now settled and to do so would be more trouble than it is worth.

ACTIVITY 5.1

- *Apply Thompson's PCS model to Stuart and Simon's situation.*

- *What do you feel are the key issues affecting Simon's, Stuart's and the staff's perception of what needs to happen following the argument?*

Comment

The incident involving Stuart and Simon has a number of levels and complexities when considering anti-discriminatory practice. For example, the difference in opinion about whether the issue is concluded highlights some of these levels, with the dominant culture – in this case the culture of the inpatient environment – being the most important consideration for the majority of those involved. This can be viewed as an example of institutional racism, a concept that was defined by the McPherson Report into the murder of Stephen Lawrence, as:

> *The collective failure of an organisation to provide an appropriate and professional service to people because of their colour, culture, or ethnic origin. It can be seen or detected in processes, attitudes and behaviour which amount to discrimination through unwitting prejudice, ignorance, thoughtlessness and racist stereotyping which disadvantage minority ethnic people.*

> (MacPherson, 1998; para 6.34)

A further definition was offered by A. Sivanandan (*Guardian*, 1999), who was at the time Director of the Institute of Race Relations, who stated that institutional racism could be understood as:

> . . . *that which, covertly or overtly, resides in the policies, procedures, operations and culture of public or private institutions – reinforcing individual prejudices and being reinforced by them in turn.*

(Sivanandan, in the *Guardian*, 1999)

In brief, Case Study 5.1 can be broken down within the PCS model as follows:

Personal Stuart believes that racist remarks in this context are normal, and now the argument is over he does not believe there are any outstanding issues to resolve.

Cultural The staff believe that the ward being settled is the most important issue, and seek to maintain this environment, seeing Simon's response as something that will create further conflict.

Structural Acceptance of the staff's position by their organisation and the wider society, which could be construed as institutional and societal racism.

The case of David 'Rocky' Bennett, in 1998, was a stark reminder of some of the discriminatory approaches and attitudes that are evident within both society and mental health services. Rocky Bennett was a 38-year-old African-Caribbean man who died as a direct result of restraint techniques used in the mental health inpatient unit where he was detained. An independent review was commissioned which found that there were numerous examples of discrimination and institutional racism to be found within the mental health system (Blofeld et al., 2003). The government issued a formal response to the report (DoH, 2005a) and initiated the 'Delivering Race Equality in Mental Health Care' programme in an attempt to tackle race inequality and discrimination.

Delivering Race Equality in Mental Health Care

Delivering Race Equality in Mental Health Care (DRE) was a 5-year action plan (DoH, 2005a) to improve access, experience and outcomes for black and ethnic minority patients and is the government's position on delivering equality in mental health. The plan recognised that statutory services need to do more to adapt to an increasingly diverse population, and to respond to the serious inequalities in mental health that evidence suggests some BME communities suffer. The programme is based on three building blocks: more appropriate and responsive services, community engagement, and better information.

The DRE programme, including the Count Me In census, has developed the Department of Health's thinking about race equality in mental health considerably since it was launched in 2005. In summary, the Department's position now is that:

- there is strong evidence of inequalities between ethnic groups in the incidence of severe mental illness (for environmental rather than biological reasons);

- there is still good evidence of inequalities in some aspects of access to services – specifically, the more adverse pathways of care that BME inpatients have followed and in the likelihood of being offered talking therapies;

- services must do more in the way they commission and provide care to tackle these inequalities, and DRE remains the blueprint for action;

- there is less strong evidence of inequalities in BME service users' experience of, or satisfaction with, mental health services, and less strong evidence of inequalities in outcomes.

Since publication of the action plan, new training modules in race equality and cultural capability have been developed for all mental health staff. These aim to improve the experience of BME service users, and evaluation of the modules has shown that patient satisfaction can improve when staff engage with the training, which suggests that the workforce is able to improve their cultural competence and capability by reflecting on their own practice and considering wider social factors that may influence the mental health status of diverse groups.

A review of the DRE programme was published in 2009 (Wilson, 2009), and this acknowledged that addressing poverty and social deprivation is key to tackling overall health inequalities, and that ethnic data and statistics alone cannot be the basis for measuring change or the quality of services. Applying the PCS model (Thompson, 2006), it is the prevalence of wider deprivation that continues to have a direct impact on cultural and individual beliefs and behaviours, and as a result discrimination can still be identified within public service provision. Practitioners need to ensure they understand the implications of these factors on the practice environment, and ultimately on the experience and treatment of those from BME backgrounds within the mental health system.

The Mental Health Act and race equality

Evidence suggests that young black men are more likely than their white counterparts to be sectioned under the Mental Health Act. The DoH has arrangements to monitor any adverse impact of the amended Act on equality for BME people, thereby meeting the commitment to the Commission for Racial Equality (now incorporated into the Equality and Human Rights Commission). However, the evidence suggests that the likelihood of being detained is still disproportionately weighted in BME communities, particularly African-Caribbean men. Several MHAC biennial reports (2005; 2009a) have considered this issue, and a further report by the Independent Police Complaints Commission (IPCC, 2008) has considered the use of section 136 detention for black males; each of these investigations demonstrated the continued high incidence, and further studies (Singh et al., 2007; Dein et al., 2007; McGrath et al., 2004) support this view. This suggests that although the overall experience of treatment may not show significant inequalities, there remains a prevailing prejudice in terms of formal powers that practitioners must be aware of and consider when applying statutory powers.

Issues discussed elsewhere in this book, such as underlying belief systems, social values and norms and social identification, all play a part in the decision making of the practitioner. This is not to suggest that all AMHP or BIA practitioners are inherently racist, but rather that risk assessment in crisis situations can be influenced by issues such as race, social resources and other demographic factors. Practitioners need to be able to challenge these norms if they are to practise in an ethical manner, and their own, service users' and the wider community's beliefs and behaviours should be examined and challenged.

Making equality and human rights real for our communities

How organisations recruit, train and promote their staff is fundamentally important to achieving the vision of equality and human rights. This means that the composition, skill and motivation of the workforce are key. Practitioners must understand the needs of the communities they serve if they are to develop practices and policies to support and enable, and ensure that services are accessible and sensitive to the needs of all people from all backgrounds. A diverse workforce – where the staff profile reflects that of the population – is critical to achieving this.

This chapter has discussed the framework within which mental health practice operates, and in order to become competent practitioners must base their decisions and actions within the legislative context. It is clear that social stigma and prejudice are still in existence, and practitioners should not seek to divorce themselves from their belief system but rather challenge the presumptions and assumptions they make, and ensure that their decisions are based on a framework of best interest and ethical practice.

In order to demonstrate ethical and value-based practice within this framework it is necessary to ensure that the whole person is considered: this includes the equality strands, each of which has an influence on how an individual experiences and understands their own situation and the services they access. The equality and diversity debate is embedded within professional practice, and anti-discrimination is a core value for the statutory mental health roles. Practitioners must ensure that diversity and differences are considered and integrated into care and support packages, and that a wider engagement with social networks and values is integral to their decisions and interventions.

Chapter summary

- Equality, diversity and human rights shape the way we understand our context and influence our beliefs, behaviours and decisions.

- The wider policy and legislative contexts for mental health practice now embed the principles of anti-discriminatory practice.

- Ensuring that the individual's whole context is considered is a core competence for the AMHP and BIA roles – diversity is present in all individuals, groups and societies and must be considered in terms of how it shapes a person's condition and presentation.

- As one of their core skills practitioners should be able to identify and evidence how these issues influence their professional practice.

FURTHER READING

Kirkbride, JB, Fearon, P, Morgan, C et al. (2006) Heterogeneity in incidence rates of schizophrenia and other psychotic syndromes – findings from the 3-center ÆSOP study. *Archives of General Psychiatry*, 63, 250–258.

McPherson, B (2008) Equality and diversity as a way of delivering the wider health and social care agenda. *Ethnicity and Inequalities in Health and Social Care*, 1 (2), 4–7.

Chapter 6

Rights and self-determination

No man is free who is not a master of himself.

Epictetus (AD 55–AD 135), Greek philosopher

Introduction

The principles of best interests and self-determination are both key to best practice in mental health service delivery. Research evidence in this area suggests that self-determination promotes recovery (Anthony, 1993; Cook and Jonikas, 2002; Carpenter, 2002), and the emphasis on equalities and human rights is wholly complimentary to these findings. The FREDA principles of fairness, respect, equality, dignity and autonomy (Joint Committee on Human Rights, 2008), as discussed in Chapter 5, provide a sound foundation for mental health practice as they place the individual central to both the decision making and the support planning processes.

The promotion of an individual's rights and choices is a core part of mental health practice, and are integral to the Codes of Practice of AMHPs and BIAs (DoH, 2008a; DCA, 2008). Practitioners therefore need to be fully aware of both the rights and choices available to individuals, and the policy frameworks and evidence base that underpin this way of working. They need to be competent and confident in promoting participation and involvement, and all staff need to be able to make decisions that may deprive an individual of their liberty while still ensuring and encouraging self-determination as much as possible. This can be difficult to reconcile, and so it is useful first to define what is meant by self-determination and to place it in the context of mental health practice.

What is self-determination?

The concept of self-determination has its roots in classical philosophy: it centres on the presumption that human development has an active tendency towards growth and integration of experiences into the sense of self (Deci and Ryan, 2002). This theory has a number of critics, who suggest that there is no inherent drive towards growth but that behavioural and personality regulation occurs as a result of environmental and social stimuli (Deci and Ryan, 2002; Williams et al., 2000). Regardless of the theory, the concept of self-determination has become embedded in social models of disability and forms an integral part of the recovery and personalisation approaches that are common in modern mental health care.

Self-determination is embedded within the Human Rights Act 1998 and the FREDA principles, and is one of the civil liberties of all individuals. The articles of the Act provide for freedoms such as liberty (article 5), privacy and family life (article 8) and expression (article 10). It gives the individual the basic right to make choices about how they live, and to self-direction, independence, and the ability to exercise their full civil rights (Cook and Jonikas, 2002; Floyd Taylor, 2006).

> *Self-determination is the ability to make informed choices for one's own life with a reasonable expectation of hope for the future . . . means being in charge of your own life, having the resources you need to create a good life, making responsible decisions that are best for you and for others around you, and choosing where, when, and how you will get support and assistance for your mental and physical health problems.*
>
> (Risser, 2003; p.209–10)

The right to self-determination is not absolute, and there are some restrictions placed upon it, for example when exercising the rights of one person impinges on or violates the rights of another (Nordgren and Fridlund, 2001), or when actions contravene legislation regarding national security or public safety (Human Rights Act 1998). This includes the impact of an individual's behaviour on the wider community, the capacity of the individual to exercise that right, and the potential harm that could occur as a result. The Mental Health Act 1983 (as amended) can be applied to restrict an individual's freedoms if they meet the criteria, in which case the individual is considered to be of 'unsound mind' under the Human Rights Act, and limitations to liberty can be applied.

CASE STUDY *6.1*

Alex is a 25-year-old man with a history of violent behaviour after drinking alcohol. Alex is arrested one Friday evening as he was verbally abusing another man in the street. On arrest he continues to be verbally abusive. At interview Alex says he has a right to drink and that he was not harming anyone, and so the police had no right to arrest him.

- *In human rights terms, what rights does Alex have?*

- *What restricts these rights?*

Although Alex does have the right to drink, his behaviour as a result violated the rights of the man he was abusing, and breached public order laws; therefore, his self-determination to make behavioural choices is the area that is being restricted.

Psychiatry, the user movement and self-determination

The debates about power discussed in Chapter 4 are particularly relevant here, as restriction of rights is a function of the imbalance of power between practitioner and individual, or between individual and society. For those with mental health problems exercising choice can be an important part of the treatment process, and self-determination is considered a key component in recovery (Anthony, 1993; Copeland, 2004; Deegan, 1996). In this context it is therefore both a basic human right and necessary for the individual's well-being, and confounds the ethical discussion about protecting both the individual and others.

The user/survivor movement in mental health is rooted in the Civil Rights Movement of the 1960s, developing alongside the Gay Liberation and the Black Civil Rights movements (MIND, 2010). During the 1970s groups began to form that were critical of psychiatry, which led to a significant shift in both how mental health was viewed and the level of involvement of individuals with mental health difficulties in service development and delivery. In this climate, the emphasis of the user movement was to question the perceived wisdom of psychiatry and challenge the restrictions and labels it placed on people (Roe and Davidson, 2005; Wallcraft and Bryant, 2003; Cook and Jonikas, 2002). Along with the emergence of the recovery model, this led to a widespread challenge to what was termed the medical model and an increase in the application of the social model to understand and respond to mental health issues (Carpenter, 2002; Crossley, 2006).

Since the early 1990s user involvement has been a significant feature in mental health policy and developments (Roe and Davidson, 2005; Cook and Jonikas, 2002), and the move towards a recovery approach, which encompasses the concept of self-determination as fundamental, has become key.

The introduction of personalisation, which began in 2007 with the *Putting People First* strategy (DoH, 2007c), and was followed in 2008 by the *Transforming Adult Social Care* circular (DoH, 2008c), has strengthened the move towards user-centred care by requiring local authorities to make significant changes to the delivery of social care. Choice and control for individuals, the key element of self-determination in this context, is one of the central foci for the future delivery of social care services, and policy direction continues to support this. Elements such as personal budgets, direct payments and greater access to services are all designed to place the individual in the driving seat of their social care. For mental health services this model is experiencing some difficulties. Issues such as the delivery of an integrated provision between health and social care (which has a different agenda), the management of risk and the delivery of safeguarding elements all need further development if a system based on self-determination is to be achieved.

Self-determination and the Mental Health Act

An AMHP has a number of powers that serve to restrict an individual's liberty and hence their self-determination. This is something that must be considered in the context of the individual's life, as such restrictions are essentially a restriction of their human rights. The Mental Health Act sets out the circumstances in which such restriction is lawful, and the Code of Practice guides the practitioner to apply the Act in a manner consistent with the Human Rights Act.

The Code of Practice explicitly requires the practitioner to consider the self-determination of the individual and to encourage their involvement as much as possible. The principles of least restriction and participation in particular make it clear that the person should be consulted and involved in decisions, and that only the minimum amount of restriction necessary is applied.

REFLECTION POINT

- *How do you ensure that the individual is consulted and involved in the decisions you make about their liberty?*

The participation principle sets out some of the ways individuals can be involved with the decisions made in formal Mental Health Act assessments, including:

- planning, developing and reviewing care and treatment, and

- involvement of carers and family members or others with an interest in the individual's welfare.

(para 1.5, DoH, 2008a)

The decision to make an application or to admit the individual to an inpatient environment may not be something that they are able to participate in, but this is only one of the decisions that is made. Decisions such as who is involved, how they are transported, which unit receives them and the treatment they will receive, are all areas where an individual's choices and wishes should be observed in order to preserve their right of self-determination within the process and ensure that the FREDA principles are applied.

CASE STUDY 6.2

James is 37, divorced, and has two children who both live with his ex-wife. He identifies himself to be of British African-Caribbean origin, as his mother and father came to the UK from Jamaica and he was born in South London. James' parents are both now deceased; however, his brother Paul lives in the area and James has a close relationship with him. James has an extensive history with mental health services and has been detained a number of times over the last 10 years. He has a diagnosis of schizophrenia and sees a CPN (community psychiatric nurse) weekly and his psychiatrist bimonthly. He is prescribed antipsychotic medication and takes this orally.

CASE STUDY **6.2** *(CONT.)*

James has recently been having difficulties with his ex-wife, as he has requested more ad hoc access to his children but she feels that his current contact routine is helpful for the children. James has become increasingly withdrawn and distressed over the last few weeks as a result of these difficulties, and has stopped taking his medication as he thinks it makes him forgetful and he feels he needs to have an alert mind at the moment. Following a night out James is arrested outside his ex-wife's house, where he was found writing with spray paint on the front wall and shouting that 'he wouldn't let her take his kids away'.

A Mental Health Act assessment is arranged and James is found to be acutely psychotic; he has several paranoid delusional beliefs about his wife and children, and is making threats to anyone who he believes is trying to separate him from his children. James discloses that he has not taken his medication for several weeks and has missed his appointments with both his CPN and his psychiatrist. The AMHP and assessing doctors agree that James should be admitted under section 3 for treatment and his care plan be re-established. James asks that his ex-wife not be informed, but wants to see his brother, and states that he does not want to travel to the hospital in an ambulance, as 'I'd rather people think I was a criminal than mad'.

ACTIVITY **6.1**

- *What are James' rights in the situation outlined in Case Study 6.2?*
- *What would you do if faced with this situation?*

Comment

Who is involved, and how the individual wants to be transported, are just two choices involved in the admission of a person to inpatient care. Although the admission itself may be against the patient's wishes, both that and subsequent treatments should be made as participatory as possible.

Under the Mental Health Act decisions can be taken in an individual's best interests where that individual is suffering from a mental disorder and it is necessary for their health and safety, or the health and safety of others. AMHPs need to be able to make an informed assessment when these circumstances present themselves and take the least restrictive action necessary to safeguard the individual and/or others. In this way the AMHP can ensure that the individual's rights and self-determination are preserved as much as possible while restrictions are in place.

Self-determination, best interests and capacity

The determination of capacity to make a decision adds an additional complexity to decisions about restriction. Where the individual has capacity they are free to make decisions that may be unwise or not in their best interests. These decisions may have legal and social consequences, but ultimately the individual has the self-determination to make that choice. Where the individual's capacity is in question, the views of family and others, and the duty of care placed on care workers, come into play, and restrictions may be placed on an individual as a result.

Under the Mental Capacity Act 2005 there is a presumption that someone has capacity unless there is something to indicate this may not be the case. The assessment of capacity is decision and time specific, and the individual must have an impairment or disturbance that is affecting how their mind or brain works (DCA, 2007). If so, the individual has to meet four key criteria to be deemed to have the capacity to make a given decision:

- ability to understand the decision to be made;
- ability to weigh the consequences of the decision;
- ability to retain the information needed to make the decision;
- ability to communicate the decision.

(DCA, 2007; p.41)

Where the individual is unable to satisfy these criteria they are deemed to lack capacity, and in these instances the decision can be made by an appropriate person in the best interests of the individual (see Chapter 9 for further discussion on capacity decisions).

Advanced decisions and advanced statements are ways in which individuals can express their wishes when they do have capacity, and these should be observed within a best interest decision, along with the views of anyone involved in the individual's welfare or who may hold lasting power of attorney. These protections exist to provide an individual with the opportunity to express their views and wishes in a way that means they will apply at times when they may not be able to make the decision themselves. To be valid the advanced decision must relate to a certain situation in which a particular treatment is refused, and when that treatment is for a mental disorder the Mental Health Act overrides the individual's decision.

CASE STUDY 6.3

On admission James is stabilised on his medication and changed to a depot injection; he refuses at the time but is considered unable to make the decision, as he had the belief that the medical team were working with his ex-wife and were trying to poison him. After a short time his symptoms start to subside, James becomes less distressed, and now understands that his medication has been changed because he had stopped taking the oral version. James discusses the injections with his doctor: he does not want to continue with the injection, stating that he will not stop his medication again without talking to someone, but will not agree to fortnightly injections. The doctor advices against this, but James states that that is his choice and goes on to record his wishes as an advanced statement on his psychiatric file. On discharge of his section 3 James reverts to oral medication.

- *What could be put in place to support James to exercise his choices?*

Comment

Once James has the capacity to make the decision regarding his medication this must be considered. His advanced decision means that he cannot be given injectable medication if he becomes ill again unless the Mental Health Act is used, and in that case the conditions of treatment against a patient's wishes must be applied, including the safeguards such as right of appeal and SOAD (second opinion appointed doctor) opinion after 3 months. Although James' advanced directive may be overruled by the Mental Health Act, it does provide him with some protection.

The Deprivation of Liberty Safeguards

The Deprivation of Liberty Safeguards (DOLS) are one further protection for individuals who lack capacity and for whom decisions are being made that deprive them of their liberty and right to self-determination. In these cases the Code of Practice (DCA, 2008) for the process makes an explicit link between self-determination and protection, stating that protections should only be applied in situations where it is necessary to protect an individual from harm, and should be for the minimum amount of time and the minimum level of restriction. The best interest assessor (BIA) role was established to allow for the independent identification of an individual's best interests and to ensure that the full circumstances are considered as part of the decision-making process (see Chapter 9 for further discussion on the DOLS process).

Although there is an acknowledgement within the DOLS process that an individual does not have the capacity to make informed decisions, this does not mean that there is no self-determination, and throughout the process practitioners need to remain aware of the views and wishes of the individual.

Restrictions on an individual's right to liberty and self-determination are used as a safeguard and protection; however, there is also an ethical debate about the balance between the dual rights of choice and protection. For mental health practitioners this can be a difficult balance to strike, and AMHPs and BIAs in particular have the statutory duty of making these decisions and ensuring the individual's rights are upheld.

The role of independent advocacy

Although mental health practitioners have a key role in ensuring that an individual's rights and self-determination are considered and observed, additional roles have been created under legislation to ensure that independent advocacy is available for those whose liberty has been restricted. These are the independent mental capacity advocate (IMCA) and the independent mental health advocate (IMHA), and they provide additional scrutiny to professional decision making specifically to ensure that the individuals' rights are upheld throughout.

These roles should be welcomed, as they provide a level of independence that is difficult for the practitioner to achieve. Practitioners may have to balance conflicting views and decisions and have an awareness of power dynamics as part of their role, and the advocacy role allows for a level of objectivity that would otherwise be unavailable.

The ethics of protection

For all mental health professionals there is a conflict that needs to be negotiated, and for AMHPs and BIAs this is more explicitly the case. In order to apply the duty of care there are times when other rights have to be impinged upon, and this creates an ethical dilemma.

In the case of an individual's self-determination this spans a range of areas, and can include a person's liberty, behaviour, expression and lifestyle choices. In circumstances that may result in restrictions being applied, the question must always be asked, is it necessary for the individual's health and safety or to protect others?

Chapter 3 discussed the social view of mental health problems, and it was concluded that public perception has a significant role to play in how potential risks are interpreted. This being the case, the practitioner needs to remain aware of these perceptions and personal values to ensure that any restrictions are necessary and not based on misconception. The decision to place an individual under restriction should always take account of the wider circumstances and the impact on their recovery.

Human rights are fundamental freedoms and should only be restricted when there are no alternatives. The use of restriction in these circumstances would be considered ethical by the teleological school of ethics, as the end result would be the primary consideration. However, this must be applied in context, and the practitioner needs to ensure that any action taken is lawful, meets the relevant criteria, and is a proportionate and necessary response. Adherence to the relevant Codes of Practice is required to ensure that practice is ethical and the use of power is not unnecessary or abusive.

CASE STUDY **6.4**

Cheryl is 63 years old and is suffering with dementia and depression. She lives alone and on two occasions has been found by neighbours wandering in the street, saying that she can't find her way home. Cheryl is very clear that she wants to stay in her own home and will accept home carers coming to help her in the morning, but no other support. She is neglecting her personal hygiene, taking her medication sporadically, and her road sense is not as good as it could be. Cheryl's family are increasingly concerned and have contacted the local mental health service demanding that she be taken into a care home, as they feel she is at risk.

- *What are the options available in Cheryl's case?*
- *Considering the dual rights of self-determination and protection, what are the ethical dilemmas for the practitioner in this case?*

Comment

Cheryl is clear that she wants to remain at home and is reluctant to accept support, so an assessment of risk and a management plan are needed to ensure that her safety and her wishes are observed. Cheryl's capacity should be assessed to ensure she is fully aware of her situation and options, and able to make an informed choice. Technological options may be useful in this case, with facilities such as telecare being possible alternative means of providing support.

Conclusion

This chapter has considered the application of restrictions to an individual's self-determination and the preservation of human rights and the FREDA principles in this context. Restrictions such as those available under the Mental Health Act and DOLS safeguards should only be applied as a last resort, and wherever possible an individual's choices and preferences must be observed.

One of the key roles of statutory practitioners such as AMHP and BIAs is to inform the individual of their legal rights, and the additional advocacy roles of the IMCA and IMHA are available to ensure that individual rights are upheld. Although practitioners are key to this process, in some circumstances decisions are made that may restrict individual rights, and in these situations an independent advocate is a useful safeguard.

Although restrictions of liberty can be considered ethical in cases where the risk cannot be managed, they should only be considered when no other options are available. Support options such as user-centred treatment planning, personal budgets and technology should be used wherever possible to minimise such restrictions. In these circumstances the role of the practitioner is to balance the rights of the individual with the need to apply safeguards, and wherever possible alternatives to restriction should be considered. Any sanctions should be applied in the spirit of participation and respect for the individual, and the use of power needs to be transparent and carefully considered.

Chapter summary

- Self-determination is a basic human right; it is only restricted when the self-determined actions of one person violate the rights of another.
- Self-determination exists within the context of the legal system, and as such there are consequences to actions that breach legislation.

- Mental health legislation allows for the restriction of individual rights in certain circumstances, and careful consideration of the individual and their context is required before any restriction is applied.

- Practitioners need to balance the dual rights of self-determination and protection and ensure that the use of power to restrict individual rights is carried out in the context of the individual and their presenting needs.

- The independent advocacy roles of IMHA and IMCA provide an additional level of scrutiny to professional practice and safeguard individual rights.

- The Codes of Practice for the Mental Health Act, Mental Capacity Act and DOLS safeguards all make explicit reference to individual rights and self-determination, and all decisions must be made in this context.

FURTHER READING

Brown, R, Barber, P and Martin, D (2009) *The Mental Capacity Act 2005: A Guide for Practice*, 2nd edition. Exeter: Learning Matters.

Department of Constitutional Affairs (2008) *Deprivation of Liberty Safeguards: Code of Practice to Supplement the Main Mental Capacity Act 2005 Code of Practice*. London: The Stationery Office.

Department of Health (2008) *Code of Practice: Mental Health Act 1983*. London: The Stationery Office.

Chapter 7
Privacy and dignity

What should move us to action is human dignity: the inalienable dignity of the oppressed, but also the dignity of each of us. We lose dignity if we tolerate the intolerable.

Dominique de Menil (1908–1997) French-American art collector and museum founder

Introduction

Privacy and dignity are key elements of practice in modern mental health; this includes a range of aspects, such as environment, communication and treatment options. Mental health practitioners need to be aware of this and actively promote individuals' rights and preferences in treatment and support situations.

As the move towards personalised and empowering services has developed, the debate about maintaining privacy and dignity, in sometimes very distressing circumstances, has increased. There have been many examples of breaches of individual rights in mental health treatment, and over the last decade significant advances have been made, including the introduction of dignity in care campaigns and the elimination of mixed-sex inpatient care.

Article 8 of the Human Rights Act 1998 sets out the individual's rights to privacy and family life, and these rights need to be upheld during treatment. The use of statutory powers does not negate the need to ensure the individual's rights in this area, and all interventions must consider and respect the individual's wishes and preferences wherever possible.

The impact of values and ethics on the practitioner's actions must encompass privacy and dignity, and this chapter will present a range of practice considerations.

A useful start to this discussion is to consider what privacy and dignity can mean in mental health settings, and to consider the values involved in some of the initiatives that have been established.

Defining privacy and dignity

Privacy and dignity are separate, yet interlinked, areas which are part of the overall culture shift towards a service provision that respects the needs, wishes and aspirations of the individual. There are a number of definitions of both terms, all relating to quality care which maintains human rights and personal respect.

Dignity combines issues such as privacy, autonomy, self-determination and respect into an overall way of interacting with people. A definition offered by the Social Care Institute for Excellence (SCIE) states that:

> *Dignity in care means the kind of care, in any setting, which supports and promotes, and does not undermine, a person's self-respect regardless of any difference.*

(Cass et al., 2009; p.6)

The Department of Health has published a range of guidance on providing services based on the principle of dignity. For example, the *Essence of Care* (NHS Modernisation Agency, 2001) defines dignity as 'being worthy of respect' (p.1) and sets out seven factors and benchmarks best practice in relation to each (Figure 7.1).

Other studies have also attempted to define what constitutes dignity in health and social care (Jacelon et al., 2004; Bayer et al., 2005; Woolhead et al., 2004), and similar themes have been identified. One example is the work of Griffin-Heslin (2005), who defined four key attributes that need to be in place to indicate that dignity is present: respect, autonomy, empowerment and communication.

Privacy as a concept has also been variously defined; the Department of Health benchmarks (NHS Modernisation Agency, 2001) define it as 'freedom from intrusion' (p.1) and Article 8 frames it broadly and includes the right to develop one's own personality and relationships with others (HRA, 1998).

The SCIE guide *Dignity in Care* (Cass et al., 2009), outlines aspects of care that are fundamental to individual privacy:

- Modesty and privacy in personal care.
- Confidentiality of treatment and personal information.
- Privacy of personal space.

(p.114)

Paying attention to these areas and ensuring that treatment observes the individual's right to privacy is a requirement of the value-based approach to modern health and social care (Cass et al., 2009; McCubbin and Cohen, 1999; James and Prilleltensky, 2002; Liegeois and Van Audenhove, 2005).

Element	Benchmark
Attitude and behaviour: • Good attitudes and behaviour. • Attitude issues are addressed. • Behaviour conveys respect.	Patients feel that they matter.
Personal world and personal identity: • Valuing and responding to diversity. • Stereotypes are challenged. • Individual needs and choices.	Patients experience care in an environment that reflects individual values, beliefs and personal relationships.
Personal boundaries and space: • Personal space respected. • Privacy achieved. • Personal boundaries identified.	Personal space actively promoted by all staff.
Communication: • Access to interpretation. • Information adapted to needs. • Appropriate records in place.	Communication takes place in a manner that respects individuality.
Privacy and confidentiality of patient information: • Informed consent sought. • Confidentiality of information.	Patient information is shared to enable care with consent.
Privacy, dignity and modesty: • Protection from unwanted view. • Appropriate and own clothing. • Modesty protected.	Care promotes privacy and protects modesty.
Availability of a private area: • Private area created. • Awareness of private area. • Risk managed for privacy.	Patients can access an area safely that provides privacy.

Figure 7.1 Essence of Care benchmarks for Privacy and Dignity
Adapted from: NHS Modernisation Agency, 2001

CASE STUDY 7.1

Kate is a 56-year-old woman with a long history of bipolar disorder. She is single and has never been married, and has a deep distrust of men. She was sexually abused by her uncle throughout her childhood and has had a number of difficult relationships with violent partners. Kate experiences severe highs and lows as part of her condition, and when high she becomes disinhibited.

CASE STUDY **7.1** *(CONT.)*

Kate has been unwell for several days and after being found by police in the town centre removing her clothing is assessed and admitted to her local inpatient unit under a section 2 of the Mental Health Act. During her stay Kate is accommodated in a mixed ward with gender-separated facilities. On her first day Kate tried to take off her clothes in the communal sitting room. The duty nurse quickly brought a robe for Kate and accompanied her into the female area, staying with her until she was calm and able to get dressed again. Kate has a single room on the ward which has en-suite facilities, and she asks the staff to call her mother to bring in her own toiletries. She also asks for some books and some clothes to be brought, and the staff arrange for this to happen the same day.

ACTIVITY **7.1**

- *What are the circumstances and actions in this case that help to protect Kate's privacy and dignity?*

Comment

There are a range of opportunities in practice to promote the privacy and dignity of individuals, and practitioners need to remain alert to how their actions can affect the service user in this respect. In the case study the staff's awareness of Kate's behaviour enables them to plan ahead to protect her dignity, and facilitating access to her own belongings helps promote personal choice and self-identity, both central elements of a dignity approach.

As Case Study 7.1 illustrates, the interactions between workers and service users can have a significant impact on the individual's view of both themselves and their options, and so a culture of respect needs to be in place to maximise the treatment and recovery processes.

Privacy and dignity initiatives

A number of initiatives have been designed to promote privacy and dignity in health and social care. These appear to have had a positive outcome on service user experiences, and further research shows that such initiatives can contribute directly to the user's sense of well-being (Swanson, 1993; Williams, 1998; Chochinov et al., 2005; Woogara, 2001; Gasper, 2004).

One of the most recent Department of Health initiatives is the elimination of mixed-sex accommodation in hospitals. The commitment to this was originally set out in 1997, the central focus being to improve the privacy and dignity of patients to ensure that individuals are comfortable, free from embarrassment and harassment, and feel safe (Howe, 2009;

Chief Nursing Officer, 2007; NHS Confederation, 2010). However, the implementation of these changes was slow, and the government relaunched the initiative in 2009 with a requirement to comply by April 2010.

In mental health terms, the issue of mixed-sex accommodation was included in the Mental Health Act Code of Practice as a requirement on hospitals from April 2010 (DoH, 2008a), and was also highlighted by the Mental Health Act Commission report in 2009, specifically in relation to women who had been detained (MHAC, 2009b) and the benefits to the individual's dignity and safety as a result of being in a single-sex environment.

The Dignity in Care Campaign is a further initiative launched by the Department of Health Care Network in 2006. Its stated purpose was:

> . . . *to stimulate a national debate around the need for people receiving care services to be treated with dignity.*

> (DoH, 2008d; p.1)

It includes a range of features such as dignity champions, actions that raise awareness of dignity in care, sharing good practice, and working towards a culture of dignified service delivery. This campaign has had a particular focus on older people; however, in 2007 the principles and good practice examples were extended to mental health, with a particular focus on tackling stigma, older people's mental health and acute inpatient care (Vaughan, 2007; Cass et al., 2009).

Evidence of outcomes from dignity activities across the country shows positive feedback from service users, with overall experiences showing improvements in areas where initiatives were in place.

Table 7.1 Good practice examples

Portsmouth City PCT

The relocation of a ward and the design of a 'dignity garden' for patients were carried out. The outcomes for the project included an increase in patient satisfaction and a calming influence on those with more difficult behaviour.

Walsall Hospital NHS Trust

A training module to improve the competence and knowledge of staff in acute settings was developed in conjunction with the local university. The module looked at mental health issues, delirium, dementia and depression, and improved staff awareness and ability to respond to patients' needs in general hospitals.

Plymouth PCT/Mental Health Partnership

A care centre was developed in Plymouth to provide health services for the local community. A café was opened in the centre, run by local mental health service users and managed by a carer. Reports from the project include service users' improved confidence.

(Sources: Opinion Leader, 2009a; Cass et al., 2009)

Many organisations and individuals have signed up to the Dignity in Care campaign and all NHS organisations are required to comply with the delivery of same-sex accommodation requirements. There is thus a greater attention and focus on privacy and dignity than has previously been the case. Practitioners need to consider these rights and values as part of their routine practice.

Privacy, dignity and statutory practice

Privacy and dignity in mental health treatment are based on the values of respecting the individual and upholding and advocating for individual rights. The Human Rights Act emphasises individual dignity, and practitioners acting in a statutory role who are in effect public authorities must ensure individual human rights are maintained. In a case that concerned the impact of health and safety regulations, His Honour Justice Munby emphasised the importance of human dignity. He said:

The recognition and protection of human dignity is one of the core values – in truth, the core value – of our society and, indeed, of all societies which are part of the European family of nations and which have embraced the principles of the Convention.

(R (on the application of A and B) v East Sussex County Council 2003)

AMHPs and BIAs are both bound by value-based Codes of Practice that focus on individual dignity and respect in practice. The Mental Health Act Code of Practice (DoH, 2008a) sets this out in all its guiding principles, particularly the principles of respect and participation. The Mental Capacity Act Code of Practice (DCA, 2007) is framed by five principles, which also guide the Deprivation of Liberty Safeguards and BIA practice, and constitute an approach that respects and supports personal dignity in situations where the individual may be unable to make decisions for themselves. All practitioners working under these Acts need to ensure that their practice considers the impact of any intervention on personal dignity.

CASE STUDY 7.2

A BIA undertakes an assessment on Deidre, a 73-year-old woman living in a residential care facility. She was diagnosed with dementia several years ago; her condition has progressed, and she moved into a residential care home 8 months ago as she was no longer able to cope at home. Deidre has periods of lucidity but can become very confused, disorientated and distressed, and this is becoming more frequent. Her daughter and son-in-law visit her once a week and she also sees her younger sister and a close friend regularly. Her

CASE STUDY 7.2 *(CONT.)*

older brother has recently died, which she is having difficulties coming to terms with. Deidre has recently started to try to leave the home, and on one occasion was found wandering in the high street. She has previously been very settled and contented in the home and has been making friends with other residents.

Over the period of a week Deidre's distress has increased and she has become agitated and confused, repeating that she has to get to her brother's to pick him up and cannot stay at the home any more, but is unable to explain the problem when asked. The staff have encouraged her to stay and have been able to calm her; however, her confusion has got worse and she is becoming more insistent on leaving. The support staff are worried, as they are not sure where Deidre will go and she is unable to retain the knowledge that her brother is dead. A deprivation of liberty approval is requested, as the staff have had to restrain Dierdre to keep her at the home.

As part of the assessment the BIA consults a range of others involved in Deidre's care. Her immediate family are concerned, but report that her brother's birthday is coming up and that he and Deidre have had an annual outing for the last 50 years, which they think might be the cause of Deidre's attempts to leave the home. The BIA talks to Deidre about this outing; it appears that she and her brother have had an annual day at the local racecourse and Deidre wants to go again. The home staff arrange for Deidre to be supported to go to the racecourse with her sister for the day, and her behaviour appears to settle as a result. A deprivation of liberty approval is then assessed to be not necessary.

When people are confused or unable to communicate clearly it may appear that behaviour is irrational or risky. The assessment process should involve all those involved in the individual's life to provide as full a picture as possible of their circumstances and wishes. In Deidre's case she was unable to articulate what she wanted, and this had resulted in an escalation of both her behaviour and the response she received. By considering Deidre's past experiences, as well as consulting with her social support network, the BIA identified a possible rationale for Deidre's change in behaviour and an action that might reduce her distress without requiring additional restrictions, all of which contributed to Deidre's personal dignity in this situation.

Where an individual may be experiencing extreme distress or behavioural disturbances it can be difficult to ensure dignity is maintained. However, much of the practice guidance on the issue suggests that attitudes, behaviours and environments can all contribute to and create a culture of dignity and respect (MHAC, 2007, 2009a; DoH, 2008a; DCA, 2007; Cass et al., 2009). These elements should be in place regardless of whether or not an individual's liberty is restricted.

Anti-discriminatory practices that promote individual rights remain a significant training focus for practitioners, and approaches that emphasise dignity have been shown to assist in both treatment efficacy (Opinion Leader, 2009b; Cass et al., 2009) and the user's experience of the service (Breeze, 1998; Gilburt et al., 2008; Appleby, 2000).

In situations that are unfamiliar, or which are not the person's choice, the way they are spoken to and treated can have a significant impact on how safe and comfortable they feel. Personal possessions, contact with particular people, or maintaining certain activities can all help the individual remain connected to their life and feel that they have a degree of control – all elements that contribute to their sense of dignity. These issues are not restricted to mental health services, but should be applied in all situations where a person enters the health and social care system.

The impact of personal and social values

Both social and personal values can have an impact on practitioner decision making and intervention, and this is also the case when considering individual rights to privacy and dignity. Individual belief systems influence behaviour directly, and so practitioners need to remain aware of potential discrimination or prejudice in their decisions and actions.

Individuals with mental health suffer from a range of stigmas and prejudices, and as a result decisions may be based on perceived rather than actual risks (Byrne, 2001; Ryan, 1998). Historically, individuals with mental health problems have variously been seen as dangerous, helpless and vulnerable, and although social understandings have progressed, some of these views have informed the development of the current mental health system.

Privacy and dignity have been a feature of mental health care for the last decade, and are concepts enshrined in the current 10-year strategy (DoH, 2009a); however, reflective challenge by practitioners of their own and others' practice is needed to combat these paternalistic approaches (Breeze, 1998; DoH, 2009a; Szmukler and Holloway, 2000; Roberts, 2004).

Anti-discriminatory practice, which is fundamental to the delivery of privacy and dignity, has been the core of the social work value base for years. Over the last decade this approach has been explicitly extended across all mental health professions, and best practice guidance, providing a competence-based approach and setting clear standards, has been applied (Hope, 2004; DoH, 2003a). The mental health statutory roles have created additional power dynamics, and practitioners need to be able to balance complex decisions about crises and risks with ensuring that individuals' rights are protected.

As discussed, social context, cultural understanding, professional knowledge, confidence and experience can all influence a practitioner's decision making, and workers need to develop the ability to assess both the individual's situation and the impact of their own beliefs and values on their response to that situation.

Comment

Everyone has their own belief system and this should not be ignored. Understanding your personal reaction to any given situation is a useful tool to guide ethical decision making. Prejudices and presumptions need to be challenged and aspects of personal dignity maintained in situations where liberty or other rights are restricted. The skill of the practitioner in these situations is to recognise the impact of their approach and the environment on an individual's sense of safety and privacy. By paying attention to the person's whole situation, the practitioner can support them in maintaining as much choice and control as possible. Supervision and training should both be available, and increased information and knowledge can assist in the reflection process, helping the worker address any beliefs that could affect their assessment and decision making.

Privacy, dignity and ethics

The emphasis on human rights, and in this case privacy and dignity, is consistent with the deontological school of ethics. However, a number of situations remain where an individual's liberty is restricted and they are treated against their wishes, and this is undoubtedly aligned with teleological thought.

The shifting focus between individual self-determination and dignity, and the more protective options of compulsion based on health and safety grounds, can mean that practitioners are required to alternate between two contrasting ethical frameworks, depending on the risk tolerances of the individual or the system. This can be difficult, and raises complex questions about the consistency of professional judgement and its impact on practice.

CASE STUDY 7.3

The mental health section experience from a carer's perspective

My son has been sectioned twice in the last 10 years. His earlier experience was more satisfactory from a medical viewpoint, and he was treated with great care and understanding, but his admission was messier.

When he was detained for the first time he was very ill but had not been engaged in services effectively, and his lack of successful treatment escalated into a formal section. As his mother I was involved in the process, as his father was no longer in contact with him. The assessment actually took place in the setting of a hospital outpatient appointment on the assumption that he would then go to the ward. They did not know my son. He refused to do this and ran off. After some time he turned up at home and was later admitted in handcuffs in the back of a police van. This was very distressing for us both, and certainly inflamed my son's belief that he was being wrongly held for a crime he had not committed. The police were respectful of me and kindly towards my son, but the actual admission was badly handled and set up tensions in the ward from the start. I recall seeing him the next day, where he stood by an almost closed window (psychiatric regulation 4 inches open only), and him saying that if he was forced to stay there he would just curl up and die. Staff did not inform him what was happening, although his ASW did, and she also supported me through this traumatic time.

After he was transferred to a neighbouring PICU the staff there ensured his privacy and dignity were respected, and he was encouraged to understand the processes of the section by reading about his legal rights. As result, he asked me as his nearest relative to request his release. It was a test of our close relationship that I felt unable to do so. In his tribunal I was allowed to give my view that he was not well enough to be discharged. This tribunal also tested our relationship, as he felt I was not supporting him but colluding with the enemy. Neither staff nor the solicitor really seemed to understand this dilemma or help me to work through it. His section had at first meant he was kept on an acute ward, but the later transfer to a PICU meant he had access to good facilities for being outside, and was generally less restricted albeit in a closed environment. Supervision was tight, and this applied to me as well. I did feel very restricted, but was supported by the staff to make meaningful visits.

On the second occasion his section had been well planned and he agreed to go to hospital, believing it was temporary. When he realised he was under a section he was angry and determined to leave. He was able to walk off the ward on several occasions because of the number of bank staff who did not know him and his legal status as a detained patient. At one point while missing he eventually phoned me, and I was put in the position of informing his social worker, who set up a police 'sting', whereby I met my son and then the police arrived as if by magic to take him back to hospital. This was a truly difficult decision for me and I felt torn between 'shopping' him, knowing he needed to be in hospital, and fearful of the potential consequences to our relationship. I was helped through this by good friends, but the professional staff seemed unconcerned or unaware of this dilemma and my anxiety.

On this ward my son was deprived of privacy and dignity. He was unable to attend occupational therapy sessions as they were held on a different ward; he was not allowed out to smoke, or to be visited other than in the main lounge. Visiting was very difficult because of the physical restrictions. The games area was banned for me, and the only quiet rooms were in the single-sex areas, so he could not meet me in the women's side and I could not meet him on the men's side! We could only see each other in the television room, which acts as the dayroom for all patients, however disturbed, and also doubled as the dining room. There was no place for us to meet for an intimate chat or to play a quiet game of cards. This meant that visiting was stressful for us both. Again we went through the tribunal process, and he strongly requested me to support his application for discharge.

Although the tribunal was held efficiently, and at the time and date set, it was almost impossible for me or his social worker to be present at regular ward rounds, as the doctors would change the times and days without discussion or notice. Clearly they felt

---

CASE STUDY 7.3 (CONT.)

that the patient was there with nothing else to do, so could be seen at any time and changes or lateness were of no consequence. This was both annoying and highly disrespectful to all concerned. I was expected to escort my son outside the ward on section 17 leave, although nursing staff were uneasy about doing this themselves because of his absconding pattern. I felt at the time that this was unfair, as I had to expect behaviour from him that others were unable or unwilling to deal with, and the level of responsibility could again have put our close relationship at risk. I also felt somewhat exploited, as I was undertaking skilled nursing tasks rather than being my son's mum.

When things went wrong I was informed only intermittently. For instance, he once locked himself in the bathroom to avoid medication, and the fire brigade were called, although I believe I could have talked him out. Once again, this would have been an example of passing the responsibility to me, but the staff had not even considered it. At no point was I well informed about his care and treatment, and neither of us was given a 'welcome' pack or introduced to a key nurse. We were not even aware that there was such a system! The values of the nursing and medical staff were not apparent in the way they treated either of us, and the loss of independence and self-determination for my son was felt by both of us.

(By Alleyn, a carer)

Conclusion

Privacy and dignity are enshrined in human rights, and practitioners undertaking statutory duties are considered to be public authorities and therefore bound to observe the requirements. Mental health legislation and policy have developed over the last two decades, and the principles of privacy, dignity and respect are now embedded within policy developments and legislative Codes of Practice. The values-based approach has extended across mental health services, and a range of guidelines have been published making privacy and dignity basic requirements in both inpatient and community settings.

Whereas mental health legislation provides the ability to enforce treatment and residency, the method by which this is achieved should be based on a participatory approach that considers diversity and personal choice. This is in line with public policy, and although the compulsory options remain, the overall ethos is one that promotes individual identity and mutual respect.

The move towards promoting privacy and dignity has been a positive one for service users, and feedback shows that an increased sense of personal dignity affects both the user experience and their general well-being. Front-line practitioners are often the key to successfully developing a culture of respect within services, and anti-discriminatory and non-judgemental practice needs to remain a focus.

Chapter summary

- Privacy and dignity are defined human rights that must be promoted within all mental health services.

- A sense of personal dignity can have a positive impact on both treatment effectiveness and experience of the service.

- The Mental Health Act and the Mental Capacity Act are both guided by Codes of Practice that explicitly set out individuals' rights to privacy and dignity, and as such AMHP and BIA practitioners need to remain aware of these issues and the impact of interventions on an individual's rights.

- Whereas restriction of liberty can affect one's privacy and dignity, attitudes, behaviours and environments can all have a positive influence on an individual, and how difficult situations are approached and managed can be significant.

- Privacy and dignity issues are wholly consistent with professional Codes of Practice, and practitioners need to retain their focus on the individual's situation and the impact of their own value base on the decision-making process.

FURTHER READING

Cass, E, Robins, D and Richardson, A (2009) *Dignity in Care: SCIE Guide 15.* London: SCIE.

Department of Health (2008) *Mental Health Act 1983 Code of Practice.* London: The Stationery Office.

Chapter 8
Effective safeguarding

The only point of government is to safeguard and foster life.

George Wald, 1906–1997, American scientist

Introduction

Safeguarding of both adults and children is an area in which all professionals have a duty, and one that has received extensive attention over the past 5 years. For mental health practitioners there is both an implicit and an explicit role here: whereas all statutory work concentrates on safeguarding the individual from harm and ensuring their rights are observed, there are also the explicit tasks of identifying potential and actual abuse and following safeguarding processes in their local practice.

Safeguarding adults and safeguarding children have different pathways, and there are pressures to link these at a strategic and policy level. Initiatives such as 'think family', which will be considered later in this chapter, are seeking greater cooperation and collaboration. However, there remains a series of silos that practitioners may need to negotiate to ensure that service users and carers are both protected from abuse and are also able to access the preventative safeguarding support before such abuse occurs.

This chapter considers the issues associated with safeguarding that may be encountered by AMHPs, BIAs and social workers in the context of mental health care. It is helpful initially to provide an overview of the requirements and policies that workers will need to be aware of, as well as local arrangements, and practitioners should ensure they know where to refer to and which teams deal with which issues in their area.

At the time of writing the change in government has resulted in many of the previous health and social care policies, including safeguarding, being under review, and it should be noted that although the principles are unlikely to change, the policy framework may see some adaptations.

Defining the terms

A number of key terms need to be stated from the outset, as workers must be aware of the remit in which they are operating in order to be able to apply safeguarding principles. These terms are described below.

- *Vulnerable* According to the NHS and Community Care Act 1990 and the Lord Chancellors Department (1997), all individuals over the age of 18 who use or are in need of community care services because of mental or other disability, illness or age, or who are unable to protect themselves against harm or exploitation, are defined as vulnerable. This includes anyone who uses mental health services, including drug and alcohol services.

- In this context all children are considered as vulnerable, and anyone under 18 years of age who is experiencing, or at risk of, abuse or harm has a right to be safeguarded by local services. The issue of consent for those aged 16–18 can create complexities, but the right to be safeguarded remains.

- *Abuse and safeguarding* Safeguarding refers to the actions taken to protect and prevent harm to individuals, both children and adults, and includes agencies and organisations working together to take reasonable measures to ensure risks are minimised (DoH, 2000; DCSF, 2010).

No Secrets (DoH, 2000) is the government policy framework for safeguarding adults and set out the definition of abuse as:

> *Abuse is the violation of an individual's human and civil rights by another person or persons. Abuse may consist of a single or repeated act. It may be physical, verbal or psychological. It may be an act of neglect or omission to act or it may occur when a vulnerable person is persuaded to enter into a financial or sexual transaction to which he or she has not or cannot consent. Abuse can occur in any relationship and may result in significant harm to, or exploitation of, the person subjected to it.*

(DoH, 2000; para 2.6, p.9)

The different types of abuse are set out in Tables 8.1 and 8.2 to assist workers in the process of identification of such situations.

Table 8.1 Types of abuse – adults

Physical Includes hitting, slapping, pushing, kicking, misusing medications, using inappropriate restraints or sanctions, burning, or any other action that deliberately causes physical harm to the vulnerable person.

Sexual Includes rape, sexual assault or attack, touching, kissing, verbal sexual comments or suggestions, exposure of body parts or showing pornographic or suggestive material, and which the person has not or cannot consent to, or has been put under pressure or otherwise coerced into.

Psychological Includes threats of harm or abandonment, coercion, deprivation of contact, humiliation, blaming, controlling, intimidation, bullying and harassment, verbal abuse, isolation or withdrawal from usual activities or contacts.

Neglect or acts of omission Includes ignoring medical or care needs, failing to provide health, social care or educational services, and withholding necessities such as medication, nutrition, hydration, heating or anything else that it would be reasonable and usual to provide for the individual's well-being.

Financial Includes theft, fraud, exploitation or pressure in respect to financial affairs, such as wills, property and inheritances, misusing or misappropriation of funds or property or possessions, including benefits.

Discriminatory Any type of abuse relating to an individual's race, gender, age, sexuality, disability, religion or belief, or gender. Can include harassment, verbal abuse, slurs, or preventing access to services or activities.

Institutional The mistreatment of an individual by a regime or staff members in an institution. Can include routines, systems or norms of the institution that deprive individuals of their rights to their preferred lifestyle or cultural diversities.

(Sources: Dakin, 2007; DoH, 2000)

Types of abuse are also set out in the guidance for safeguarding children; however, there is no central definition of what constitutes abuse: rather, this is defined in terms of significant harm and the impact of the environment and/or the actions of others. The policy framework *Working Together to Safeguard Children* (DCFS, 2010) draws on the Children's Act 1989 and 2004, stating that children should be safeguarded and their welfare protected to ensure they are:

- protected from maltreatment;

- the impairment of children's health or development is prevented; and

- they are growing up in circumstances consistent with the provision of safe and effective care.

(para. 1.20; p. 34)

There is a great deal of policy and guidance regarding safeguarding, and in the case of children a clear legislative framework in place. These arrangements are different for adults and children, and the following sections will provide an overview of each framework, and how mental health practice should be applied within each.

Table 8.2 Types of abuse – children

Physical Includes hitting, shaking, kicking, punching, scalding, suffocating, and other ways of inflicting pain or injury on a child. It includes giving a child harmful substances, such as drugs, alcohol or poison.
Emotional When a parent or carer behaves in a way that is likely to seriously affect their child's emotional development. It can range from constant rejection and denial of affection, through to continual severe criticism and deliberate humiliation.
Neglect The persistent lack of appropriate care, including love, stimulation, safety, nourishment, warmth, education and medical attention.
Sexual When a child or young person is pressurised, forced or tricked into taking part in any kind of sexual activity with an adult or young person. It includes encouraging a child to look at pornographic magazines, videos or sexual acts.

Note: Bullying and domestic violence can also be forms of child abuse
(Source: NSPCC, 2009a)

The policy framework: safeguarding adults

The Department of Health *No Secrets* guidance, which was published in 2000, required all local authority areas to have policies and Codes of Practice for multi-agency safeguarding arrangements in place by 2001. Prior to this guidance agencies and professionals working with vulnerable groups had a generic duty of care; however, this was not always coordinated, and working arrangements between the various agencies were not consistent across geographical areas.

Safeguards in relation to the regulation and standardisation of care were introduced by the Care Standards Act 2000. This piece of legislation introduced standards and regulation for registered care providers, established the National Care Standards Commission (NCSC), which had powers to register and inspect all care homes and independent hospitals, introduced registration for social care workers and the establishment of the General Social Care Council (GSCC), and introduced a central list, the Protection of Vulnerable Adults (POVA) list, of individuals who should not be allowed to work with vulnerable people. Although these regulations had some gaps, including issues such as the fact that only social workers are currently registered, and that submissions to the POVA list cannot be made by the NHS, the introduction of centralised regulation and minimum standards represented a significant step forward in the safeguarding agenda.

The Safeguarding Vulnerable Groups Act 2006 further developed the regulations and registration requirements of individuals who work with vulnerable people, and were largely based on the recommendations of the Bichard Report (Table 8.3). This was an inquiry set up to consider the child protection processes in Cambridgeshire and Humberside following the case of Ian Huntley, who in 2003 was convicted of the murders of Jessica Chapman and Holly Wells. The inquiry particularly considered data collection, vetting of staff and information sharing.

97

In 2009 the Independent Safeguarding Authority (ISA) was established as required under the 2006 Act, and at the time of writing is under review by the new government. If fully implemented, all individuals working in regulated activities (i.e. having access to vulnerable people, children or adults) will be required to be registered with the ISA. It will be a criminal offence to work if barred, or to employ an individual who is either not registered or known to be barred.

Table 8.3 The Bichard Report

Key recommendations:

- The introduction of a national police intelligence data system across England and Wales, and a new Code of Practice for information management to ensure records are kept for the right amount of time.

- Guidelines to be published to inform agencies when they should involve the police in allegations and abuse investigations.

- CSCI inspections to include the review of decisions to not inform the police.

- Training for all professionals undertaking investigation.

- Police inspections to include vetting systems and processes.

- Clearer guidance on CRB checks and who should have enhanced or standard disclosures.

- A central registration scheme for workers who have contact with vulnerable adults and children.

Additional legislative provisions are also included in the Mental Capacity Act 2005 and the subsequent Deprivation of Liberty Safeguards, which were introduced by the Mental Health Act 2007 (see Chapter 10 for further discussion). In relation to adults without capacity to make decisions, two new offences were introduced: ill-treatment and willful neglect, which allow for the prosecution of individuals who have caring responsibilities but who neglect or withhold that care. The Deprivation of Liberty Safeguards introduced legal protections for individuals in hospitals or residential care, and established the new role of best interest assessor, to provide an independent view and recommendations on the application of care and treatments that deprive an individual of their liberties under the Human Rights Act 1998.

REFLECTION POINT

- *What types of activities or actions could have an impact on an individual's rights or liberties?*

- *Are these activities or actions also abusive, and if so, what type of abuse are they?*

In October 2008 the Department of Health (2008e) published a consultation document reviewing the *No Secrets* guidance and considering changes that could be made to strengthen the safeguarding framework. The consultation considered the introduction of legislation comparable to that regarding the safeguarding of children, and asked for feedback on a number of areas, including how to keep people safe and maintain the vision of independence, choice and control.

The outcome of this consultation was published in July 2009 and 12,000 responses contributed to the review, 3000 of which were members of the public to whom the guidance might be applied. The key findings were as follows:

- Safeguarding requires empowerment, and the victim's voice needs to be heard.

- Empowerment is everyone's business, but safeguarding is not.

- Safeguarding adults is not the same as child protection.

- The participation and representation of people who lack capacity is important.

(DoH, 2009f; p.13)

The overall conclusions were that there needed to be greater involvement and participation of those individuals at risk of abuse or exploitation, and that this requires greater cooperation between agencies and ownership by all those involved; also that people do not want to be treated like children or be subjected to the same system as that which governs children's safeguarding. The government has since set out its next steps in the reform of safeguarding adults (DoH 2010), which include an interdepartmental ministerial group to set the policy and priorities, new legislation to place local safeguarding boards on a statutory footing, and the production of new guidance and professional toolkits in the autumn of 2010.

REFLECTION POINT

- *How do you ensure that safeguarding activities are also empowering and respect the individual's independence and choice?*

The policy framework: safeguarding children

The framework for child protection is based on the Children's Act 1989, which has since been superseded by the Children's Act 2004, and the associated guidelines and policy, most notably *Working Together to Safeguard Children,* which was originally published in 2006 and revised in 2010 (DCSF, 2006, 2010), *Every Child Matters* (Chief Secretary to the Treasury, 2003) and the guidance concerning the *Children's Plan* (DCFS, 2007). All of these place a duty on services to cooperate to ensure that safeguarding activities are coordinated, and that they are set out within an outcome framework for children and young people.

Every Child Matters outcome framework

- **Being healthy** Enjoying good physical and mental health and living a healthy lifestyle.

- **Staying safe** Being protected from harm and neglect.

- **Enjoying and achieving** Getting the most out of life and developing the skills for adulthood.

- **Making a positive contribution** Being involved with the community and society and not engaging in anti-social or offending behaviour.

- **Economic well-being** Not being prevented by economic disadvantage from achieving their full potential in life.

(Chief Secretary to the Treasury, 2003)

The principle of all of the safeguarding children requirements is that society has an inherent duty to protect the young, and that the needs and welfare of the child are paramount. For health and social care agencies this is embedded within all service delivery, and as such mental health practitioners are required to consider the family circumstances and the needs of any children in that family when working with the adult, regardless of what that adult's relationship is with the child.

Recent safeguarding incidents have had a significant impact on mental health services. The death of Victoria Climbié in 2000, which led to her guardians Marie-Thérèse Kouao and Carl Manning, being convicted of murder, resulted in an independent inquiry concerning the systemic failure of services to safeguard her welfare, and the first Laming Report was published in 2003; this included a range of practice recommendations for improving communication, information sharing, record keeping and inter-agency collaboration. The death of Peter Connelly (Baby Peter) in 2007 was a case in Haringey where a range of services were involved but failed to prevent his death, and subsequently his mother pleaded guilty to causing or allowing the death of a child (Haringey LSCB, 2009). The subsequent reviews by Lord Laming (Laming, 2009) and the Care Quality Commission (CQC, 2009) have helped focus the attention of all health and social care agencies on their responsibilities to safeguard children, regardless of their primary care or treatment purposes, and reinforced the need for multi-agency cooperation and communication.

At the same time as these reviews were published the National Patient Safety Agency (NPSA) issued a rapid response alert (NPSA, 2009). This followed the National Confidential Inquiry into Suicide and Homicide (2006), which reviewed 254 homicide convictions between 1997 and 2004 in cases where children were murdered by their biological parent or step-parent. The review found that in 37% of cases the parent who committed the offence had a diagnosed mental health issue, including depressive illness or bipolar affective disorder, personality disorder, schizophrenia, and substance or alcohol dependence (NCISH, 2006). This is supported by reviews into serious case reviews (Ofsted, 2008) which indicated that 28% of cases involved an individual with a mental health problem. This information must be considered carefully, as there are many millions of individuals with mental health difficulties who are excellent parents, and it should never be presumed that the two are directly linked; however, there are some indicators (see Table 8.4) that practitioners need to be aware of.

Table 8.4 NPSA – Preventing harm to children by parents with mental health needs

This guidance placed a requirement on organisations providing services to adults with mental health problems to implement the following:

- All assessment, CPA monitoring, review and discharge planning documentation and procedures should prompt staff to consider whether the service user is likely to have or resume contact with their own child or other children in their network of family and friends, even when the children are not living with the service user.

- If the service user has or may resume contact with children, this should trigger an assessment of whether there are any actual or potential risks to the children, including delusional beliefs involving them, and drawing on as many sources of information as possible, including compliance with treatment.

- Referrals should be made to children's social care services under local safeguarding procedures as soon as a problem, suspicion or concern about a child becomes apparent, or if the child's own needs are not being met. A referral must be made:

  o If service users express delusional beliefs involving their child, *and/or*

  o If service users might harm their child as part of a suicide plan.

- Staff working in mental health services should be given clear guidance on how to make such referrals, including information sharing, the role of their organisation's designated lead for child protection, and what to do when a concern becomes apparent outside normal office hours.

- A consultant psychiatrist should be directly involved in all clinical decision making for services users who may pose a risk to children.

- Safeguarding training that includes the risks posed to children from parents with delusional beliefs involving their children or who might harm their children as part of a suicide plan is an essential requirement for all staff. Attendance, knowledge, and competency levels should be regularly audited, and any lapses urgently acted on.

(NPSA, 2009)

This guidance makes the explicit links for mental health professionals that have currently been balanced and considered within the realm of professional judgement. It can present a challenge to practitioners, as the main safeguarding consideration is always the child, even though the primary service user may be the adult, and has required policy changes within organisations to encompass the information-sharing and assessment requirements that now form part of the overall policy framework.

> ### CASE STUDY *8.1*
>
> *Sharon is a single mother with two children aged 8 and 12 who has anxiety and depression. Her husband moved out approximately 6 months ago, but still sees the children on a weekly basis. Sharon attacked her husband on a number of occasions, requiring police*

intervention. She was arrested on charges of assault 6 months ago, but her husband did not press charges, and this led to his moving out. Sharon's father lives on the same street; he is 86 years old and has poor mobility. Sharon and her 12-year-old daughter care for him, providing meals and domestic chores.

After her husband left Sharon became very withdrawn and low, and has told her CPN that she thinks her children and her father are telling her husband that she is not coping, and that he is going to come and take her children away while she is sleeping.

Social services became involved with the family following Sharon's arrest when the police contacted the service, and a children and family team social worker is supporting the children. Sharon regularly sees her psychiatrist and CPN, and a social worker from the older people's team is involved with her father. A direct payment has been arranged for him to employ a home carer for his personal care needs.

ACTIVITY 8.1

- *What does the CPN need to be aware of, and who does she need to liaise with?*

- *Should a referral to the safeguarding team be made on this information? Please state why/why not.*

Comment

The mental health assessment should consider the whole family, including the various responsibilities, both parental and informal. Additional family or social support should be considered, and the level of support/nature of the relationship between Sharon and her husband needs to be considered.

The needs of the children should be a consideration: is Sharon providing for their needs? The children and families team should be involved in this, and should be aware of the wider context of the children, for example education engagement, general health and behaviour.

The CPN should involve the psychiatrist as a matter of routine in the care and support planning process, and risk assessments should consider the wider context as well as Sharon's individual situation.

Identifying abuse

There are a range of indicators and risk factors that may suggest that abuse is taking place or has the potential to take place. However, these are not guarantees or certainties, and practitioners need to be able to assess the situation and use their judgement to intervene effectively. In addition, in the case of adults the issue of consent can create additional complexities, and there are many instances in health and social care where an adult abuse individual chooses to remain in the abusive situation; in these instances workers will need to support and manage the risks rather than intervening directly.

Possible indicators of child abuse

- A child who is often bruised or injured, often very dirty or smells, who is often hungry, or under- or over-dressed.
- A child who is often left at home alone or who is left in unsafe situations, or without medical attention when they need it.
- A child who seems very afraid of particular adults and reluctant to be alone with them, or who is often very withdrawn from others.
- A child who has unexplained changeable emotions, such as depression, anxiety or severe aggression.
- A child who shows sexual knowledge or behaviour inappropriate for their age.
- A child who is growing up in a home where there is domestic violence or who is living with parents or carers who are involved in serious drug or alcohol abuse.

(Source: NSPCC, 2009b)

In adults, the signs and symptoms are less easy to define, and can include bruising or injury, a deterioration of physical and mental health that is not in line with the usual symptoms or parameters of the individual's condition (Lachs and Pillemer, 2004), changes in financial situation, or money going missing that cannot be explained by the individual (Pritchard, 2007). Changes in behaviour also need to be explored (Lachs and Pillemer, 2004; Pritchard, 2007); however, in mental health terms, where symptoms fluctuate and levels of distress change regularly, these can be less easy to identify.

Carer stress can be a key risk for adult abuse (Grafstrom et al., 1993; DoH, 2008f; Beach et al., 2005) and workers need to assess the family situation carefully. The National Carers Strategy (DoH, 2008f) and carer legislation – such as the Carers (Recognition and Services) Act 1995, the Carers and Disabled Children Act 2000, and the Carers (Equal Opportunities) Act 2004 – all place a duty on social care and health bodies to assess the needs of individuals undertaking caring roles. Providing support for these roles and helping them maintain their outside interests appropriately can make a real difference and minimise the risk to the well-being of both carer and the vulnerable person (DoH, 2008f).

CASE STUDY *8.2*

Graham is a 29-year-old man who has a diagnosis of schizophrenia; he has had several hospital admissions over the last 5 years as he has experienced psychotic episodes. He is currently quite stable but is continuing to see his social worker at the CMHT who is supporting him.

Graham lives with his father, who is experiencing poor physical health at the moment. Usually Graham's father makes sure that he takes his medication and attends his appointments, but he is currently finding this increasingly difficult and is getting angry when Graham asks him for help.

Graham goes to see his social worker and tells her that his dad keeps shouting at him, and that he cannot remember whether he has taken his medication that day but can't ask his dad.

REFLECTION POINT

- *What would you suggest or put in place in this situation?*

Comment

Graham and his dad usually have a good relationship; however, his dad is finding it difficult to cope at the moment and needs some support, both with his own health and help to continue to support Graham. Carer breaks, increased visits or tele-health devices are all options in this situation, and such interventions may reduce his dad's stress and prevent the relationship deteriorating.

So far this chapter has presented the policy framework and various definitions of safeguarding and abuse. The remainder of the chapter concentrates on how the safeguarding agenda fits into mental health practice, and will consider issues such as consent and the ethical dilemmas that can be presented by safeguarding issues, in particular how AMHPs, BIAs and mental health practitioners can negotiate these areas to ensure that safeguarding becomes an integral part of practice.

Assessing and treating children

In adult mental health practice practitioners may be working with someone who has or lives with children, or in the case of AMHPs the worker may be called upon to undertake an assessment of a child who is particularly disturbed or presenting a risk as a result of a mental health problem.

Whereas the Mental Capacity Act 2005 excludes under-18s, the Mental Health Act 1983 does not, and AMHPs need to become competent to undertake assessments on adolescents, including being aware of how to access local support to inform their decision making.

The Mental Health Act 2007 made some key amendments to the Mental Health Act 1983 and the revised Code of Practice (DoH, 2008a) in terms of 'age-appropriate' assessment and treatment, which recognised that the needs of children are different from those of adults, and encompassed the issue of safeguarding.

The 'age appropriate' legal requirements

Section 131a, Mental Health Act 1983 (as amended by Mental Health Act 2007):

- For any patient under the age of 18 years who is liable to be detained, or who is admitted to hospital

  (i) The hospital managers must ensure the environment is appropriate and suitable for the patient's age, and

  (ii) The hospital managers must consult a person who has knowledge of, or experience with, patients under the age of 18 years.

Code of Practice – Chapter 36 (DoH, 2008a):

- One of the three professionals (either one of the doctors or the AMHP) should be a practitioner specialising in child and adolescent mental health (CAMH); where this is not possible a CAMH practitioner should be consulted as soon as possible (para 36.20).

- A patient aged 16–18 years, who has capacity, should be treated as per s131. This means that the person themself consents to informal admission. Parental consent in this situation is not considered to be valid on its own and the individual's consent should always be sought (para 36.38–36.50).

- For under 16s the 'Gillick Criteria' (also known as the Fraser Guidelines) should be applied to determine whether a person has capacity to consent (para 36.38–36.50), and can be admitted and treated informally if they are competent to make that decision.

General principles for the treatment of children are set out in the Code of Practice (DoH, 2008a). These are connected to the safeguarding children frameworks, and include acting in the best interest of the child, involving them as much as possible and seeking their views, and ensuring the minimum intervention necessary is used.

In terms of the age appropriateness of the environment, the Code states that this pertains to both facilities and trained staff, but also to a routine that enables the continuation of personal, social and educational development and gives equal access to educational opportunities as their peers. These considerations are consistent with the outcome framework set out in *Working Together To Safeguard Children* (DCSF 2010).

One further point regarding the arrangements for under-18s is that the logistics of having one of the three assessors as a CAMH practitioner may be difficult in some areas. Where this is the case AMHPs need to be aware of how to access advice from a CAMH practitioner in their area.

Carrie is 16 years old; she has been detained under section 136 and taken to a local place of safety after being found by the police on the roof of a multistorey car park, threatening to jump off. She has had no support from the CAMHs service, but has recently been to see her GP. She has evidence of recent self-harming on her forearms and is refusing to eat or drink. Carrie says she does not want to live any more. The AMHP contacts the GP, who says that Carrie has been depressed recently and having problems at school; he has made a referral to CAMH but the appointment has not yet been made for her to see someone. He also says that he considers Carrie to have the capacity to make decisions about her care and treatment. Carrie's mother and father both arrive and want to be involved in the assessment. Carrie is saying she will not talk to the AMHP with her mother in the room. Her parents say that they want Carrie to go into hospital as she needs help.

ACTIVITY *8.2*

- *What are the consent issues in Carrie's situation?*
- *If Carrie refuses to be admitted what would your options be?*
- *What would the AMHP need to do as part of undertaking this assessment?*

If Carrie has the capacity to make the decision she would need to consent to admission, and her parents' consent does not change this requirement.

The guiding principles of the Act would need to be applied, and as an individual able to make decisions Carrie's wish for her mother to leave the room should be upheld.

If she is to be admitted her age would need to be considered, as well as her education, wishes and preferences. When deciding where she should be admitted, the AMHP would be required to consult a CAMH practitioner.

Assessing and treating parents and families

There will be many occasions when the family context affects both the assessment and treatment or support options for individuals experiencing mental health difficulties. As already discussed, carer stress can have a detrimental effect on a person's well-being, and can also be the case with parents (Nicholson et al., 1998; Oyserman et al., 2000; Kerkorian et al., 2006). The AMHP may therefore need to negotiate between the well-being of the parent and the best interests of the child, and this can be difficult. The complexities are compounded by societal attitudes to parents with mental health difficulties (SCIE, 2009a; Aldridge and Becker, 2003; Nicholson et al., 2001). Research in this area has demonstrated that attitudes to parents with mental health problems and the availability of services can have a negative effect both on the appropriateness of the support individuals receive to maintain their parental role (Brunette and Dean, 2002) and their willingness to engage with services (Nicholson et al., 1998, 2001).

The importance of parental mental health has been recognised by the government and is a public mental health priority. It has also been identified in the *New Horizons* strategy (DoH, 2009a), which makes explicit reference to the support that should be available for families and to help promote positive outcomes for both parents and children. Treating parents effectively under the Care Programme Approach is a stated priority area for the delivery of mental health services, and is seen as the method by which outcomes can be improved.

> *. . . interventions promoting maternal mental health, parenting programmes, home visiting and early education programmes result in improved mental health for both parents and children, with improved child outcomes impacting on school and community environments.*

(DoH, 2009a; p.35)

When undertaking assessments, especially at times of crisis, practitioners need to remain aware of children or other vulnerable adults that may be within the home or who rely on the individual for support. The system, of which the person is part, cannot be discounted in the decision-making process, and as the Code of Practice makes explicit in the guiding principles of respect and participation (DoH, 2008a; para 1.4–1.5), the whole circumstance of the person should always be fully considered.

REFLECTION POINT

- *When undertaking an assessment how do you make sure you consider the family and ensure the well-being of any children in the household?*

One initiative that has been launched to promote the coordination of services to adults and children is the *Think Family* programme (DCSF, 2008) developed by the Department of Children, Schools and Families, with cross-government support as a response to research by the Social Exclusion Taskforce which found that families facing multiple disadvantages, such as mental health problems, poor housing, poverty and unemployment, were achieving poorer outcomes despite better outcomes across the rest of society. The report went on to state that adult services were not taking full account of the implications for the family when difficulties such as mental health problems arise (Social Exclusion Taskforce, 2007). What this means is that workers in adult services will need to think wider than the impact on the individual and take into account the whole family.

Examples of the 'think family' approach include:

- Assessments that consider the needs of other family members and how these affect the individual's needs.

- Working with other local agencies to identify, refer and plan how to meet the needs of the wider family.

- Seeking specialist support when multiple or complex needs are identified, and implementing a whole-family support plan.

- Agreements over information sharing.

(DCSF, 2008)

It should be noted that any indicators of abuse or that the family situation is a significant risk should be referred to the appropriate safeguarding team.

Applying safeguarding adults processes in AMHP and BIA practice

Safeguarding principles and processes should be evident in all mental health support, as all service users whether in general or statutory practice areas, are considered vulnerable. Local area arrangements define how referrals should be made and to whom, and AMHPs will need to be aware of these processes as well as the overall safeguarding principles.

The roles of AMHP and BIA are safeguards in themselves, and both are concerned with ensuring that an individual's rights and best interests are protected. As already discussed, the worker needs to consider the wider family and informal support networks as part of the decision-making process, and identify significant others in the individual's life, in order to understand their context and consider the risks.

Suspected incidents of abuse should be recorded and referred to the appropriate local authority team as soon as possible; however, the issue of consent is also a consideration. As discussed in the policy framework section of this chapter, one of the key findings from the *No Secrets* consultation was that adults did not want to be treated in the same way as children, and so although the worker should alert the local authority, the adult has the right to remain in the potentially abusive situation if they have the capacity to make that decision. This can create an ethical dilemma: the worker may need to balance their duty of care with the knowledge that abuse is occurring, and this can be a difficult situation to reconcile. Risk minimisation and support mechanisms may be the appropriate option in some cases, and workers will need to negotiate carefully with the vulnerable person, and in some cases their families, to implement protection plans that are acceptable to the person involved.

CASE STUDY *8.4*

Andy is currently in police custody after being arrested for breaking the windscreen of a car parked outside his local pub. He is 24 years old and has a diagnosis of personality disorder. He has been known to mental health services since he was 19, and is seen regularly by his psychiatrist and a CPN. When Andy was brought to the police station he became very distressed, saying that he hated his family and didn't want to live any more. The police surgeon examined him and found bruising on his arms and neck, and said that Andy might be at risk of harming himself, so a Mental Health Act assessment was arranged.

The AMHP attends the police station to see Andy; she asks him some questions and finds out that the car he smashed belonged to his brother, and that the bruises happened when he was fighting with his brother. The AMHP contacts the CPN, who tells her that there have been a couple of occasions when Andy has told him that he and his brother had fallen out recently.

After Andy calms down, the AMHP feels that he doesn't meet the criteria for admission under the Act; however, when told he is not going to be taken to hospital Andy becomes

---

distressed again, saying he cannot go home as his brother will hurt him. The AMHP decides to investigate the situation further as she does not feel comfortable with what Andy is saying. Andy's nearest relative is his mother, and the AMHP makes contact with her. She is unwilling to talk about Andy's brother, but does say that he has recently returned home and can be a bit hard on Andy at times.

The AMHP speaks to Andy again who discloses that his brother moved back to the family home about 2 months ago and has hit Andy several times after he has been out drinking. Andy says he does not want to tell anyone but does not want to go home tonight.

ACTIVITY *8.3*

- *As the AMHP on Andy's assessment, what options would you consider?*

- *Would you make a referral to your local safeguarding team?*

A referral to the safeguarding team should be discussed with Andy and his consent sought; if he is unwilling to consent the AMHP may still need to make the referral and log the incident.

Andy is asking for alternative accommodation for the night, and depending on local services this may or may not be an option – the AMHP would need to decide whether the circumstances were severe enough to be eligible for social care support, and to consider what could be put in place for Andy when he returns home, which he is saying he wants to do.

The involvement of the family, particularly his mother, needs to be explored, and speaking to the brother may be an option, although this would need to be discussed with Andy.

Conclusions

This chapter has considered the two agendas of safeguarding adults and safeguarding children, and the policy frameworks and complexities within which mental health practitioners operate and how they should be applied in practice.

Safeguarding adult processes are part of all practice, and practitioners should be aware of the systems and processes, as well as the service user's rights. Direct intervention in risk situations may not always be an option, but the overall aim is to support the individual, help them to protect their rights and minimise risk in any potentially abusive situation. There are many ways this can be achieved, from assisting the individual to take direct action, or in cases of criminal activity involving local police, through to providing alternative care or accommodation or increasing community support. AMHPs and BIAs may not be involved in providing these supports directly, but they may be required to mobilise appropriate support and refer on to other services, and so will need an awareness of the principles and knowledge of local area arrangements. Do you know your local services and referral pathways?

In the case of child protection it is explicit what action must be taken, and in cases where there is suspected abuse the practitioner must alert the relevant authorities and cooperate with any actions carried out. In cases where there is a child in the environment and a parental mental health issue, support should be provided to both the parent and the child. The AMHP may be the worker that identifies family issues, or who is called on to assess parents or children with a view to hospital admission, and as such they need to be aware of their responsibilities under both the Mental Health Act and the safeguarding children frameworks. They will also need to be aware of the local resources, where specialist advice can be sourced, and how to make referrals to children's services. Do you know your local services and referral pathways?

Chapter summary

- Both children's and adults' safeguarding require multi-agency communication, cooperation and joint working.

- Safeguarding is an integral part of mental health practice.

- AMHPs and BIAs have a safeguarding function in their roles.

- The Codes of Practice for mental health and mental capacity both rest on safeguarding and best interests principles.

- Assessments should take account of the family and its members.

- Assessments should be informed by specialist advice in complex cases.

- Safeguarding issues and risks can have a profound impact on mental health, and mental health issues can increase these risks.

- Carer and family support should be considered as a mechanism to support the individual.

- Practitioners need an awareness of local systems and referral routes.

FURTHER READING

DoH (2000) *No Secrets: Guidance on Developing and Implementing Multi-Agency Policies and Procedures to Protect Vulnerable Adults from Abuse.* London: DoH.

Although the consultation documentation (DoH, 2008e; 2009f) provides an update on the safeguarding adults policy, this is not yet compiled into final guidance and so the 2000 publication remains the main source.

Department of Children, Schools and Families (2010) *Working Together to Safeguard Children.* London: DCSF.

This is the most up-to-date policy guidance on the safeguarding children requirements at the time of writing.

SCIE (2009) *Think Child, Think Parent, Think Family: A Guide to Parental Mental Health and Child Welfare.* SCIE Guide 30. London: SCIE. Available at: **www.scie.org.uk/publications/guides/guide30**.

Provides an overview of the *Think Family* model and its benefits within mental health support services.

Chapter 9
Capacity

The right of each individual in any relation to secure to himself the full benefits of his intelligence, his capacity, his industry and skill are among the inalienable inheritances of humanity.

Leland Stanford (1824–1893) American tycoon, politician and founder of Stanford University

Introduction

An individual's capacity to make a decision is a core consideration in mental health practice, and professionals need to be equipped to make assessments regarding an individual's capabilities. In previous years decisions and the circumstances in which they could be overridden were embedded within the framework of common law. In this context a professional could act in an individual's best interests where they believed that individual was unable to make an informed decision for themselves. This arrangement was termed 'the common law doctrine of necessity', and provided that mentally incapacitated adults could be restrained using reasonable force and given treatment without consent, if it was necessary in their best interests.

The Mental Capacity Act 2005 came into force as a phased implementation between April and October 2007, and was further amended by the Mental Health Act 2007 in regard to the deprivation of an individual's liberty. This legislation was drawn up in response to what was known at the time as the 'Bournewood Gap' (see the case summary below).

Case summary: HL v United Kingdom (Bournewood)

HL was a 49-year-old man who suffered from severe autism, challenging behaviour, and was unable to communicate. In 1994 he went to live with carers, Mr and Mrs E, under a resettlement scheme from Bournewood Hospital where he had lived for 32 years. HL attended a day centre once a week as part of his placement. In 1997 HL was readmitted to Bournewood Hospital as he had become agitated and was attempting to harm himself. HL was compliant and was admitted informally. Mr and Mrs E were denied access to visit HL and discharge was refused by the hospital; they subsequently took legal action in relation to his detention.

The case appeared in the High Court, which ruled in favour of Bournewood Hospital. The Court of Appeal overturned the ruling and found that the admission was unlawful, as *'had he attempted to leave the hospital, those in charge of him would not have permitted him to do so'* (R v Bournewood). Only those who had the capacity to consent could lawfully be given psychiatric inpatient treatment without the formal measures of the Mental Health Act 1983. The NHS trust that provided Bournewood Hospital challenged this ruling, with support from the Department of Health. The case was heard by the House of Lords, which ruled that the admission was lawful as a compliant mentally incapable individual could be treated under the common law doctrine of necessity.

In October 2004 the case was heard by the European Court of Human Rights (ECHR), which held that HL had been deprived of his liberty. He had no recourse to the protections offered by the Mental Health Act 1983 (such as the ability to challenge detention and the restrictions on treatment). The absence of procedural safeguards and the lack of access to the court amounted to a breach of the following articles of the Human Rights Act 1998:

> *5 (1) Everyone has the right to liberty and security of person. No-one shall be deprived of his liberty save in the following cases and in accordance with a procedure prescribed by law.*

> *5 (4) Everyone who is deprived of his liberty by arrest or detention shall be entitled to take proceedings by which the lawfulness of his detention shall be decided speedily by a court and his release ordered if the detention is not lawful.*

> (45508/99 (2004) ECHR 471)

This judgement was a landmark in the treatment of individuals who lack capacity, and the implications for health and social care commissioners and providers were significant. At the time of the ruling there were an estimated 50,000 patients in residential care and 22,000 in hospitals (DoH, 2005b) who were deemed incapable of consenting to their admissions. As a result the government issued a consultation document and response to the HL case considering options that could be used to address the 'Bournewood Gap'.

The Mental Capacity Bill was at this time already in parliament, having been introduced in June 2004 prior to the ECHR judgment. The Bill introduced a framework for the assessment of capacity and the application of best interests, as well as creating a new advocacy role in the form of the independent mental capacity advocate (IMCA) and a new court of protection. The Bill received Royal Assent in April 2005; however, the lack of safeguards available for incapable yet compliant patients, as identified in the ECHR case, were not fully addressed by the legislation. As a result, provisions were added to the Mental Health

Act 2007 to amend the Mental Capacity Act 2005 and create a legislative framework that provided protections in cases of deprivation of liberty.

This chapter sets out some of the key elements and safeguards of the mental capacity and deprivation of liberty provisions, and encourages the practitioner to consider their decisions within the context of this legislative framework.

Values and the principles of the Mental Capacity Act

As with the Mental Health Act, the Mental Capacity Act rests on a set of principles that must guide any considerations or actions taken within it. These are:

- **A presumption of capacity** Every adult has the right to make his or her own decisions, and must be assumed to have capacity to do so unless it is proved otherwise.

- **The right for individuals to be supported to make their own decisions** People must be given all appropriate help before anyone concludes that they cannot make their own decisions.

- Individuals must retain the right to make what might be seen as unwise decisions.

- **Best interests** Anything done for or on behalf of people without capacity must be in their best interests.

- **Least restrictive intervention** Anything done for or on behalf of people without capacity should be the least restrictive of their basic rights and freedoms.

(Section 1, MCA 2005)

The central principles of the mental capacity legislation, including the Deprivation of Liberty Safeguards, are linked to those embedded within the Human Rights Act 1998. This mirrors the European Convention of Human Rights, and provides protection for the basic rights and freedoms. Article 5, the right to liberty and security, and Article 8, the right to respect for private and family life, are particularly relevant when considering an individual's capacity to make decisions about their lives, although other articles may also be applicable.

These principles require the practitioner to question not only the capacity of the individual to make the relevant decision, but also their own values. This is necessary to ensure that assessments and any subsequent decisions are based on an objective judgement of an individual's best interest, and not unduly influenced by the practitioner's own values. This is particularly the case with decisions and actions that are against the predominant social norms and behaviours, as discussed in Chapter 3.

Assessing capacity

The individual's capacity should be assessed when there is cause to question whether they understand the situation or decision to be made: the Mental Capacity Act 2005 and the subsequent Code of Practice (DCA, 2007) set out the framework for this. Capacity is a time- and decision-specific concept: there is no legal basis for a global capacity statement, and because an individual is unable to make a decision about one aspect of their lives does not suggest they lack capacity in other areas.

There are two stages to determining capacity: first, does the individual have a mental impairment or disturbance of the mind or brain, and does this mean they are unable to make the decision concerned at the specified time?; and second, does the individual:

- Have a general understanding of what decision they need to make and why they need to make it?

- Have a general understanding of the likely consequences of making, or not making, this decision?

- Understand, retain, use and weigh up the information relevant to this decision?

- Are they able to communicate their decision (by talking, using sign language or any other means)?

(DCA, 2007; p. 41)

For AMHPs undertaking a Mental Health Act assessment, this should be a core part of the assessment process. Considering whether detention is required should also take into account the individual's ability to consent to informal measures. The principles of the Mental Health Act set out requirements to consider the least restrictive alternative to admission and to ensure participation, and so the AMHP needs to have a sound grasp of whether the individual being assessed understands the actions and measures that may be taken. For an informal admission to be carried out, consent needs to be considered, and where the individual does not have capacity it may be appropriate to facilitate an admission under the Mental Capacity Act 2005 (DoH, 2008a; paras 4.13–4.22) rather than to apply a formal detention under the Mental Health Act. The AMHP needs to have an awareness of both legislative frameworks and the accompanying Codes of Practice to ensure that the principles of least restriction and purpose are fully considered in each case.

Deprivation of Liberty Safeguards

The process for authorising deprivations of an individual's liberty are overseen by what are termed 'supervising authorities': in the case of social care establishments these are local authorities, and in the case of health care environments and hospitals the local Primary Care Trust. Deprivation under these safeguards is only lawful in cases where it is in the best interests of the person to protect them from harm: it is a proportionate action in direct relation to the potential for harm if the deprivation is not undertaken, and if is there is no less restrictive option available (DCA, 2008; Jones 2009).

There are two types of authorisation that can be put in place: an interim or emergency approval and a standard approval. Interim approvals are for a period of 7 days and are enacted by the managing authority – the establishment or organisation where the individual is resident. These must only be used where immediate deprivation is required, and where a delay would present a significant risk of harm to the individual. During this period the managing authority must make an application to the supervising authority for a standard approval, for which six assessments are required. Table 9.1 and Figure 9.1 set out the assessments required and the process of applying for a deprivation of liberty request.

Table 9.1 Assessments undertaken in Deprivation of Liberty process

Age	The person is over the age of 18 years.
Mental health	The person is suffering from a mental disorder as defined in s1 of the MHA (assessor must be a section 12-approved doctor under MHA).
Mental capacity	The person does not have the capacity at this time to make this decision (as set out in the MCA 2005).
Eligibility	The person is eligible to be assessed under DOLS (is not subject to detention or leave under the MHA and the purpose of detaining is not partly or solely for mental disorder treatment, for which the MHA would apply).
No refusals	The DOLS does not clash with any advanced or substitute decisions made by a donee under a lasting power of attorney or deputy appointed by the court of protection.
Best interests	The deprivation is in the person's best interest to prevent significant harm to themselves, and it is proportionate to the likelihood and severity of the potential harm.

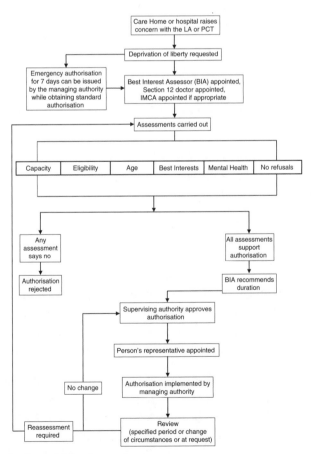

Figure 9.1 Deprivation of Liberty process

The definition of what actually constitutes a deprivation of liberty is an area that practitioners must carefully consider. The act of locking a door to prevent exit may not itself be a deprivation. However, if it is not proportionate to the likelihood or severity of potential harm, or is combined with other factors, it may constitute a deprivation of the individual's liberty (Jones, 2008).

> The difference between deprivation of liberty and restriction upon liberty is one of degree or intensity. It may therefore be helpful to envisage a scale, which moves from 'restraint' or 'restriction' to 'deprivation of liberty'. Where an individual is on the scale will depend on the concrete circumstances of the individual and may change over time.

(DCA 2008; para. 2.3)

The guidance from the Department of Health is that professionals and providers must ask themselves the following:

• Does the care and/or treatment being provided take away the person's freedom to do what they want to do to the extent that they are being deprived of their liberty?

• Do you believe that the care and/or treatment is in the person's best interests?

(DoH 2008g; p.3)

The Code of Practice for the safeguards sets out some examples that may constitute a deprivation (para 2.5, DCA 2008), including factors such as level of staff control over daily contact, and continual supervision. There is also a small number of case law examples that considers the definition and can assist in guiding decision making in this area; several of the key cases are detailed below.

Defining deprivation of liberty – summary of relevant case law

HL v UK (2004)

HL was deprived of his liberty under Article 5 when he was admitted informally. A key factor was that the healthcare professionals treating and managing him exercised complete and effective control over his care and movements in a period when he was under continuous supervision and was not free to leave.

Storck v Germany

The applicant had on several occasions tried to leave the hospital. She had to be shackled in order to prevent her absconding, and had been returned by the police on one occasion. She was also unable to maintain contact with the outside world. A query was raised regarding whether she consented to confinement. The Court found that the applicant had not, or could not, consent to her continued stay, and as such was deprived of her liberty.

JE v DE and Surrey County Council (2006)

JE was a 76-year-old man suffering from dementia. He repeatedly asked to go home with his wife, and the County Council refused. JE's wife brought a legal claim seeking a declaration that the County Council had deprived her husband of his liberty under Article 5, and of the right to family life under Article 8 of the ECHR. The judge found that the husband had been deprived of his liberty, as the restriction was not temporary and JE was restricted from leaving.

LLBC v TG (2007)

TG was a 78-year-old man with dementia and cognitive impairment. TG was resident in a care home, but was admitted to hospital with pneumonia and septicemia. While he was in hospital, there was a dispute between the local authority and TG's daughter and grand-daughter about TG's future. The council obtained an order from the court, directing that TG be delivered to the care home identified as appropriate by the council. That order was subsequently changed and TG was able to live with his daughter and granddaughter. TG's daughter and granddaughter claimed that the period of time he had spent at the care home amounted to a deprivation of his liberty.

The judge considered that there was no deprivation of liberty in this case, but it was bor-derline. The key factors in his decision included:

- The care home was an ordinary care home where only ordinary restrictions of liberty applied.

- The family were able to visit TG on a largely unrestricted basis and were entitled to take him out for outings.

- TG was personally compliant and expressed himself as happy in the care home. He had lived in a local authority care home for over 3 years and was objectively content with his situation there.

- There was no occasion where TG was objectively deprived of his liberty.

It is clear from these examples that although the Codes of Practice provide guidance for the decision maker, this is not exhaustive. The professional must consider the whole con-text to determine whether a deprivation has been, or needs to be, applied to safeguard the individual from harm.

REFLECTION POINT

Considering the information discussed, what types of situation would you consider as a deprivation of an individual's liberty?

Comment

The level of control exercised over the individual's daily life is a critical consideration: a single restraint or restriction is not sufficient to constitute a deprivation, and the practi-tioner needs to consider the whole circumstance in order to reach a judgement.

The role of the Best Interests Assessor

When undertaking assessments under the Deprivation of Liberty Safeguards, a minimum of two assessors are required – a mental health assessment is undertaken by a section 12-approved doctor (MHA, 1983) and the other assessor must be a professional qualified to undertake the best interest assessment. Specific training and approval is required for this role, and this assessment is central to the decision-making processes under deprivation of liberty arrangements.

The best interest principle is set out in the guiding principles of both the Mental Capacity Act and the deprivation of liberty Codes of Practice; it states:

> *If a person has been assessed as lacking capacity then any action taken, or any decision made for, or on behalf of that person, must be made in his or her best interests.*

(MCA 2005; Principle 4)

Determining what is in an individual's best interest is complex, and the Codes of Practice (DCA, 2007; DCA 2008) provide some guidance; however, the practitioner must consider the circumstances of each individual they assess, taking into account issues such as any anti-discriminatory concerns, the context and situation of the individual, including how they are involved in the decision, whether they are likely to regain capacity, the views and wishes of those involved, and the previous wishes of the person themselves (DCA, 2008; SCIE, 2009b).

Making decisions in an individual's best interest is not a new concept; however, this was the first piece of legislation to formalise the principles. Previously the concept was enshrined in common law and based on the rulings and decisions of the courts. Family involvement was often at the discretion of the professional; however, the capacity measures have created a legal duty to consult and consider the views and wishes of significant others (Williamson, 2007), a significant step forward for the rights of carers and families.

The role of the Independent Mental Capacity Advocate

The Mental Capacity Act 2005 is the first piece of legislation that gives a statutory right to advocacy (Gorczynska, 2007). Under the Act, local authorities (LA) and NHS Primary Care Trusts (PCT) have a duty to ensure that independent mental capacity advocates (IMCAs) are available to anyone who does not have an informal representative and who is subject to decisions or actions under the capacity legislation (Jones, 2008). This role is seen as an important safeguard for individuals, providing support and representation, and ensuring that the Mental Capacity Act is being followed. Like BIAs, IMCAs undertake specialist training and are independent from the services providing care and treatment.

The legal right to advocacy is another important development in terms of safeguarding individuals' human rights. The power imbalance and legal sanctions within mental health care have historically been in favour of the professionals, and this framework represents a landmark shift in the focus of that control. The Mental Health Act amendments followed this trend, and the 2007 Act created a similar role for those subject to formal sanctions – the independent mental health advocate (IMHA). With a similar remit – in this case to ensure the Mental Health Act is followed – the IMHA provides representation and support for those within the civil compulsory treatment system (Jones, 2009).

This protection of rights is invaluable in terms of the empowerment agenda, and roles such as the AMHP and BIA have an important function to safeguard. However, these roles are still occupied by professionals who are subject to the pre-existing power dynamic between user and worker. The IMCA and IMHA roles on the other hand provide an external scrutiny and representation that has not previously been afforded to those who may be unable to voice their own concerns and challenges. As such this should not be underestimated in terms of the political shift towards service user self-determintion within the health and social care system.

Advanced decisions, deputies, power of attorney and the Court of Protection

As well as creating specific roles and advocacy duties, the capacity legislation provides an additional suite of safeguards for the individual that the practitioner must be aware of and integrate into their practice.

Advanced decisions have for a number of years been a consideration in both mental health and palliative care; however, the Mental Capacity Act provides a legal status for these decisions. Previously known as advance statements and living wills, the advantage of an advance decision is that it places a legal status on prior decisions made by individuals with regard to medical treatment. The decision can be either verbal or written, and relate to treatment they do not wish to be administered in certain circumstances should they become incapable. Medication, ECT or other medical interventions can be specified, and where these are in place the professional must not override the decision. The decision can include life-sustaining treatment, but must be within the law: for example, assisted suicide could not be a valid advanced decision (DCA, 2007; Jones, 2008). It should be noted that with the exception of ECT or psychosurgery, in certain situations advanced decisions may be overridden by the Mental Health Act, and AMHPs and other practitioners need to ensure that individuals are aware of this possibility.

The Enduring Power of Attorney Act 1985 was amended by the Mental Capacity Act 2005; under the original legislation, when an enduring power of attorney (EPA) was appointed the nominated person could make decisions regarding property and financial matters where the individual no longer had the capacity to manage their own affairs. The Mental Capacity Act replaced these provisions with lasting powers of attorney (LPA), which extended the role to personal welfare, which can include health decisions. An individual can now choose one or several attorneys to make different decisions for them in specified areas. The role of the LPA is to make the decisions that they feel the person would make if they had capacity, rather than the decision the LPA themselves would make, and this is an important part of this protection. To be valid, the appointment of an LPA must be written and registered with the Court of Protection. When a lasting power of attorney comes into effect the views and decisions of the attorney must be adhered to except in certain cases – these are in relation to life-sustaining treatment (where this is not explicitly specified in an LPA), deprivations of liberty, or consent to treatment under the Mental Health Act (DCA, 2007; Jones, 2008).

The Court of Protection has several duties under the capacity legislation: it registers and regulates the lasting power of attorney provisions, and where necessary it can appoint a deputy to make decisions on behalf of the person lacking capacity. It can also make judgements, decisions and prescribe actions that must be taken to safeguard the individual where there is a particularly complex issue, conflicting opinions, or no suitable representation for the person to assure their rights are being observed and protected (DCA, 2007). It is a specialist court and has the same status as the High Court.

Advanced decisions can be valid regardless of the format, and the practitioner needs to evidence how these are identified and considered within the assessment and care planning processes; the involvement of others in these processes is also vital to ensure that the whole situation, including the views of any appointed individuals, is considered.

Interaction between the Mental Health Act and the Mental Capacity Act

In the majority of cases the Mental Capacity Act is seen as a less restrictive option than formal detention under the Mental Health Act; however, this does not mean that it can be reverted to as a matter of course. Where the criteria for the Mental Health Act are met, these measures should be used, and indeed in most cases the sanctions of the Mental Health Act override those of the Capacity Act. Both are Mental Health Statutes, despite the difference in focus, and in many areas there are overlaps (Fennell, 2008; Jones, 2009; 2008). Mental health care practitioners need to ensure they are well versed in the provisions of both and must be able to act in accordance with the principles of both Codes of Practice. AMHPs in particular should consider whether the individual has capacity as part of the Mental Health Act assessment, and if not, what measures or safeguards they can apply to ensure the guiding principles are applied.

CASE STUDY 9.1

Sarah has a diagnosis of bipolar disorder and is well known to mental health services. She states that she has spent the last 4 days using crack cocaine and heroin continually, and hasn't slept or eaten. She has presented to the A & E department with cut arms and legs and will not say what happened. On assessment Sarah is slurring her words, has unsteady gait, and is repeating the phrase 'help me, they're coming'. She is obviously distressed. She is refusing medication to calm her down, and the attending doctor is stating that she does not have capacity to take this decision; the A & E nurse is not convinced that this is the case, and her care coordinator says that she usually has capacity to take decisions regarding her treatment.

ACTIVITY 9.1

- *Does Sarah have capacity to make decisions about her treatment at this point?*

- *Does Sarah meet the criteria to be assessed under the Mental Health Act?*

- *What factors should be considered?*

Comment

Capacity is a fluctuating state and incapacity can be temporary. In Sarah's case this is a possible scenario; as a result, actions that are not immediately necessary should be postponed and time allowed for her to regain capacity. Under the Mental Health Act capacity should be a consideration – if Sarah is intoxicated she cannot be assessed, and time must be allowed for intoxication to wear off before a decision is made. Sarah's immediate safety and welfare should be considered: is her health or safety at risk, or are others at risk at this time and in this environment? If the answers to these questions are no, then the course of action would be to ensure she is comfortable and to wait for her to regain capacity.

Conclusion

This chapter has provided an overview of the values and safeguards of the legislative framework for mental capacity, including the areas where it interacts with the Mental Health Act. The interface between these two statutes is complex and the practitioner may need to consider both areas. From a values perspective these two pieces of legislation are consistent with human rights freedoms, and place a duty on services and professionals to embed their decision making within an ethical and values-driven context.

Involvement and consultation are central when making decisions concerning compulsion. Where previously professionals have been able to make a decision which was, in their opinion, in the best interest of the individual, regardless of previous decisions or the present context, this has now shifted and the service user, or their nominated deputies, now have powers that cannot be overridden. This represents significant progress towards the aims of choice and control for the individual, and upholds articles 5 and 8 of the Human Rights Act 1998 by challenging the power dynamics between individual and professional in a way that has not previously been seen.

As discussed in Chapters 2 and 3, social values, norms and attitudes inform what is seen as ethical and effective in the treatment of mental disorder, to an extent that is not experienced in other service user groups; however, individuals (and their carers) now have various formal safeguards outside the Mental Health Act that can enable a legitimate challenge to the professional view and empower individuals to exercise more control over their situations, even in times where they do not have the capacity to make decisions for themselves.

Chapter summary

- Capacity is a time-specific, decision-specific assessment and global presumptions about an individual must not be applied.

- Capacity can be a fluctuating state.

- There is an interface between capacity and the Mental Health Act, and the decision regarding the legislative framework to be used should be made according to the individual's needs and the least restriction necessary.

- Involvement and consultation are best practice regardless of the individual's capacity, and tools such as advanced decisions are useful.

- The Mental Capacity Act and DOLS safeguards are set within a value base and recognise the need for personal dignity and respect.

FURTHER READING

Department of Constitutional Affairs (2007) *Mental Capacity Act 2005 Code of Practice.* London: TSO.

Department of Constitutional Affairs (2008) *Deprivation of Liberty Safeguards: Code of Practice to Supplement the Main Mental Capacity Act 2005 Code of Practice.* London: TSO.

Chapter 10
Complex needs

CHAPTER OBJECTIVES

This chapter will assist readers in meeting the following mental health national occupational standards as relevant to all professional groups, including the statutory roles of AMHP and BIA under mental health and mental capacity legislation.

- D4 Work with individuals to identify their needs, related risks and the need for intervention.
- G13 Promote peoples' rights and encourage them to recognise their responsibilities.
- J1 Work with people to identify their needs for safety, support and engagement and how these needs can best be addressed.
- J3 Enable people who are a risk to themselves and others to develop control.

We struggle with the complexities and avoid the simplicities.

Norman Vincent Peale (1898–1993), Protestant preacher and author

Introduction

This chapter considers some of the complexities that are evident in practice for individuals who have traditionally been viewed as the more complex service users, including the impact of prejudices on practice, the legislative context, and appropriate treatment and service availability. Research evidence has shown that prejudice and stigma, both within and outside the system, can have a significant impact on the treatment and outcomes of individuals with complex difficulties (DoH, 2002; Banerjee et al., 2002; Sayce, 2001; DoH, 2009a; NSIP, 2009; RCP, 2009).

Two specific areas are considered here: substance misuse and personality disorders (including deliberate self-harm); however, the principles explored can be applied to any marginalised or socially excluded group. Value judgements and ethical considerations are acutely evident when dealing with complex difficulties, and AMHPs, BIAs and mental health practitioners are all required to consider how both societal and individual views affect decisions and actions.

The case of substance misuse in practice

The Department of Health *Dual Diagnosis Good Practice Guide* (DoH, 2002) was published as part of the overall mental health policy implementation guidance. Its focus was to locate the ownership of care and treatment within mainstream services firmly with specialist input and joint work with substance misuse teams as required. Historically this service user group has been passed between services, with both psychiatry and addiction services claiming it was the others' responsibility; the 2002 publication, and subsequent guidance (DoH, 2006c), stated that this had long been the case and needed to be addressed. Unfortunately, the guide had no enforcement powers, and the interpretation and degree of implementation are patchy and dependent on local views and arrangements.

There are a great many differences between how mental health and substance misuse services are managed, and there is an inherent conflict in the philosophies of each which can become a barrier to providing coherent and consistent care. Other difficulties include a lack of training and awareness of the issue, pessimism about positive outcomes, rigid service boundaries, and a lack of clarity in the roles of different services and professionals (Rethink and Turning Point, 2004; Turning Point, 2007).

CASE STUDY 10.1

An AMHP assesses a young man who agrees to attend the local drug service for assessment and treatment if he is not admitted, and states that his mental health care coordinator can monitor his attendance and level of engagement.

For this to be appropriate and best practice, the AMHP would need to determine a number of things prior to making the decision, including:

- *Does the local drug service provide a service to those with a mental health issue, and is the man eligible to receive these services?*

- *Does the local drug service have a protocol with the mental health service that allows for the sharing of information to the agreed level, and if it does not, can one be arranged?*

- *Is there a waiting list at the local drug service? How are referrals received and prioritised, and are there fast track criteria that could be applied to this case?*

In some areas specific dual diagnosis services are being created to provide support to mental health services and AMHPs; however, this is not the case in all areas, and AMHPs need to consider whether there are local services that can be drawn upon as an appropriate treatment option for service users presenting with dual diagnosis problems.

The Mental Health Act and substance misuse

The amendments to the 1983 Act created by the Mental Health Act 2007 have maintained the exclusion criteria that an individual does not meet the definition of a mental disorder by reason of drug and alcohol dependence, and section 3 of the 2007 Act states that for the purposes of Section 1 (definition of mental disorder):

Dependence on alcohol or drugs is not considered to be a disorder or disability of the mind. [For the purpose of the Act]

However, this does not preclude those who have coexisting substance misuse and mental health issues from being subject to assessment under the Act, or those who are presenting with a mental disorder as a result of the use of drugs, for example drug-induced psychosis (DoH, 2008a; para. 3.8–3.12).

The prevalence of drug and alcohol misuse is estimated at between 22% and 44% for psychiatric inpatients (Philips and Labrow, 2009), and so this is an area that the AMHP is likely to encounter.

Trying to determine whether presenting symptoms are due to mental disorder or substance use is often difficult, and practitioners require a basic understanding of how the two areas interact in order to inform their decision making.

Dual diagnosis or coexisting mental health and substance misuse issues can be placed into four categories (DoH, 2002):

1. A primary psychiatric illness precipitates or leads to substance misuse.

2. Substances make the mental health problem worse/alters its course.

3. Intoxication and/or substance dependence leads to symptoms.

4. Substance misuse and/or withdrawal leads to symptoms or illnesses.

The extent to which a substance can cause or affect a mental disorder or its development is variable and will change over time. The two issues are often so interlinked that it is impossible to identify where one begins and the other ends.

Despite the range of possible presentations, research (Banerjee et al., 2002) has highlighted a number of common factors that can be applied to this group, regardless of the type of mental health issue or substances used. These include:

- increased likelihood of suicide;
- more severe mental health problems;
- homelessness and unstable housing;
- increased risk of being violent;
- increased risk of victimisation;
- more contact with the criminal justice system;
- family problems;
- history of both sexual and/or physical childhood abuse;
- more likely to slip through gaps in services;
- less likely to be compliant with medication and other treatment.

(Banerjee et al., 2002; p.3)

This service user group is particularly vulnerable, and these are some of the key risk factors that the AMHP will need to consider when undertaking their assessment. The previous

Mental Health Act Code of Practice required that the assessing practitioners take all relevant factors into account, and the amended Code of Practice requires the same consideration (paras 4.5–4.7, DoH 2008a). As such, AMHPs need to retain an awareness of how far-reaching coexisting mental health and substance misuse issues can be and their potential to affect the individual's presentation, functioning and access to services.

Assessment

It is explicit within the law that an assessment under the Mental Health Act should not be carried out with a service user who is intoxicated, unless their behaviour or the urgency of the situation creates a genuine risk (DoH, 2008a; para. 4.55). However, unless the individual is incoherent, or otherwise obviously intoxicated, this may not be a straightforward judgement: many of the symptoms seen in mental health conditions are similar to those of some substances.

Table 10.1 Symptoms of mental illness and substance misuse

Mental health presentation	Substances with similar presentations
Hypermania Grandiosity Hyperarousal Obsessive–compulsive behaviours Disinhibition High mood	All symptoms of possible stimulant use, including amphetamine, and crack or powder cocaine Also possible symptoms of hallucinogen use, particularly Ecstasy
Low mood Low energy and lethargy Apathy	Symptoms of alcohol use, cannabis use and chronic use of benzodiazepines
Paranoid ideation Delusional beliefs	Symptoms of high levels of cannabis use, also other hallucinogenics, for example LSD, and created by consistent use of stimulants
High expressed emotion	Symptom of Ecstasy use, as well as possibly alcohol, cannabis and stimulants
Aggression Somatic symptoms Sleep deprivation Disturbances of eating/drinking	Stimulant and alcohol use Also symptoms of substance withdrawal
Hallucination	LSD, magic mushrooms, cannabis and high levels of stimulant use

Note: The effects of drugs and alcohol can vary depending on many factors, including the person, their weight, gender, general health, levels of tolerance and metabolism, as well as dosages and strengths of the substance used.

It is clear from this comparison that the commonality in presenting symptoms is signifi-cant, and the service user may be unwilling to disclose whether they have been using substances.

In order to apply best practice the AMHP will need to consider the presentation and all available information, and ask themselves following questions:

- Is the service user disclosing the use of substances?

- Are the relatives/carers indicating a use of substances?

- Is there any known history of the use of substances?

- Are there any visible signs of substance use, for example dilated pupils or injection marks?

- Could the service users' presentation be solely as a result of substance use? If so, what evidence suggests this?

CASE STUDY 10.2

You are the duty AMHP and are called to the local police station to assess a 32-year-old man who has been detained under section 136. The police doctor has seen the man and tells you that he suspects drug use, but that the man is not intoxicated. He was detained after being found wandering around a local park singing to himself; a member of the public called the police and when officers arrived the man lay on the floor in the foetal position, sobbing, and saying that he needed someone to look after him.

- *What information do you need prior to seeing the man?*

- *What are your initial considerations?*

When you see the man he has scarred lower arms that are consistent with injection, and tells you that he needs his prescription. He confirms that he is a user of the local drug service and that his worker's name is Keith; he also tells you that he has never been to see anyone from mental health services.

- *What information do you now need in order to make an assessment?*

- *Who would you contact?*

You contact the drug service and speak to Keith, who provides you with the following information. The man has a 10-year history of heroin and alcohol use and has previously taken at least two serious overdoses. He was referred to mental health services but the referral was rejected – the primary issue has always been drug use. He usually presents with low mood and some paranoia. He has a history of non-compliance with prescribed medication. His next of kin is listed as his mother, but he has refused to allow information to be shared with her in the past.

- *What is your next step?*

- *What issues influence your assessment and why?*

- *What options are available in your local area?*

Your risk assessment and the doctor's assessment are not consistent. You feel that the man poses a significant risk to himself and feel that his presentation is one of helplessness and hopelessness, with a clear indication of depression and possible suicidal ideation. The assessing doctors agree with the risk assessment, but one states that although he feels the man meets the criteria of mental disorder and would be willing to make the required recommendation, he should not be admitted as he believes it is a drug-induced presentation.

- What factors would you need to consider?

- What is your next step?

- What additional information is required?

- Would you make an application for compulsive treatment?

Comment

This case could be argued in terms of both detention and community input, and there is no right answer. The AMHP in this case needs to ensure that they have considered all available information and the local services that are available as a key part of their decision-making process.

Summary of key issues – substance misuse

The AMHP needs to be aware of a number of key issues when assessing an individual with the dual issues of substance misuse and mental health difficulties:

- The term dual diagnosis is often used by health and social care services: it is a label with which to identify a group of service users and is not an actual diagnosis. The range of issues that the coexistence of mental health and substance misuse problems can create is very broad, and can affect all areas of an individual's life.

- The prevalence of coexisting mental health and substance use issues is common, with an estimation of 44% of the psychiatric population using some type of non-prescribed substance.

- The use of substances does not exclude service users from assessment under the Mental Health Act unless there is no evidence of a mental disorder. The symptoms of both mental disorder and substance misuse can be similar, and the AMHP and assessing doctors need an awareness of both areas in order to make an informed judgement.

- Services vary greatly across geographical areas, and the AMHP needs to be versed in what is available in their area in order to consider the range of community options and hence apply the principle of the least restrictive option.

- The interaction between mental health and substance misuse is complex, and often the two are so intrinsically linked it is impossible to identify the progression pathways.

- The stereotypical views of this service user group and the often preconceived ideas of the professionals involved are often not objective, and should be considered within the wider context of the individual's presentation and psychosocial circumstances.

- The risks associated with this service user group are significant both in terms of the health and safety of the individual and the protection of others; however, unwise or antisocial behaviour is not enough in itself to apply formal provisions, such as those under the Mental Health Act, but do require comprehensive and evidence-based assessment of risk factors in each case.

The case of personality disorders in AMHP practice

The issue of assessing and treating individuals diagnosed with personality disorders is especially complex. Although these individuals are usually deemed vulnerable in social care terms, and as such entitled to assessment and services under the NHS and Community Care Act 1990, for health colleagues the eligibility for service is based more upon the ability to treat, and the effectiveness of treatments for personality disorder is controversial within the mental health system (DoH, 2003b; Bateman and Fonagy, 2000; Linehan et al., 1991; Kernberg and Michels, 2009; Widiger, 2008) .

In 2003 the Department of Health published a policy implementation guide called *Personality Disorder: No Longer a Diagnosis of Exclusion* (DoH, 2003b). This was drawn up to support the inclusion of personality disorder within the National Service Framework (DoH, 1999a), and to provide guidance to commissioners and providers on best practice for this group of service users. The main components of the 2003 guide (p.6) were:

- To improve access to appropriate services.

- To deliver appropriate offender services alongside offending behaviour interventions.

- To ensure that education and training equipped workers to deliver competent assessment and management of individuals with personality disorders.

A significant issue at this time was the lack of services able to provide appropriate services. As a result, those with personality disorders were largely treated on the edge of the mental health system – via accident and emergency departments and the criminal justice system, rather than in a defined service or model of care. The closure of generic social work or vulnerable adult teams within social service departments and the establishment of specialist teams, integrated with health colleagues, led to further marginalisation, as the boundaries of specialist team remits largely excluded them from receiving a consistent service from statutory agencies except during times of crisis.

The policy guide clearly stated that specialist multidisciplinary teams were to be established alongside mainstream mental health services, and local PCT areas were tasked to commission the most appropriate provision for their areas. This has led to a lack of consistency across the country in the development of and investment in complex needs services. In some areas specific teams are available; in others in-reach teams have been established to support community mental health teams (CMHTs). There are many variations of service model, and AMHPs need to be aware of the resources in their local area.

At the same time as service models were developing, the mental health legislative reforms were also being debated. The Mental Health Act 1983 did allow for the assessment of individuals with personality disorder where there was evidence of seriously irresponsible or abnormally aggressive behaviour; however, the requirement of detention under section 3 of the Act was that the condition was 'treatable', a term that was heavily debated and gave rise to a plethora of case law (for examples see R (Wheldon) v Rampton 2001; R (N) v MHRT, 2007; R (P) v MHRT East Midlands and North East Region, 2002).

One of the central controversies of the Mental Health Bill, which finally led to the amendments of the Mental Health Act 9 years after the reforms were first raised (see Chapter 2) was the application to those with what were seen as 'dangerous and severe personality disorders'. The amendments introduced by the final manifestation, which became the Mental Health Act 2007, and which constituted a significant compromise to the original proposals, included an expansion of the definition of mental disorder which can be applied to personality disorder. Section 1 (2) of the amended Act now states that mental disorder means *any disorder or disability of the mind*, and the criteria for detention/compulsion for treatment has been changed from *treatability* to *appropriate medical treatment is available* (s3 (2) (d)). These amendments have broadened the use of the Act to more easily encompass personality disorders, as the requirement for seriously irresponsible or abnormally aggressive behaviour has been removed and those with personality disorder fulfil the criteria for mental disorder in the same way as mental illnesses such as schizophrenia and bipolar disorder. Although these changes make formal sanctions more accessible, they do not mitigate the complexities, variances in treatment efficacy, or the wide range of circumstances that apply to this group, or provide guidance as to how practitioners should navigate these in their decision-making processes.

Complexity and personality disorder

A number of different personality disorders have been identified, and along with their associated symptoms they are listed in the psychiatric diagnostic manuals DSM–IV (APA, 1994) and ISD-10 (WHO, 1990). These are clustered into three categories according to their common themes:

- Cluster A Suspicious

- Cluster B Emotional and impulsive

- Cluster C Anxious

Difficulties with social relationships, personal identity and dysfunctional coping mechanisms are common factors through all of the disorders, and as a result an individual's support networks may not be very robust. An individual with personality disorder is much more likely to present to services in response to a specific event or social crisis, and so the assessor needs to have an awareness of the whole circumstances and the difficulties common to this group.

Some of the common themes from the research in this area include an increased likelihood of drug and alcohol misuse, an increased likelihood of a history of abuse, self-injury, unstable housing, transient relationships, and risk-taking behaviour (DoH, 2003b; Skodol et al., 2005; Reich and Green, 1991). In addition, those with personality disorders are more susceptible to comorbid mental health conditions, such as depression, anxiety, eating disorders and suicidality (Reich and Vasile, 1993; Shea et al., 1992; Garno et al., 2005), which can adversely affect the outcome of treatment for other mental health conditions.

The issue of stigma and discrimination is an area that is particularly relevant with individuals diagnosed with personality disorders, and one that needs to be considered in assessments. From a values-based perspective individual workers must be aware of their own prejudices and their implications. Research has shown that mental health professionals are as likely to have stereotypical beliefs and make assumptions as anyone else, especially with regard to social acceptance (Nordt et al., 2006; Wahl and Aroesty-Cohen, 2009). This can be further compounded by a prejudice against those diagnosed with personality disorders, who are seen as highly demanding and attention seeking (Treloar and Lewis, 2008; Bowers and Allen, 2006), and as a result the assessment process needs to be reflective and address any preconceived ideas on the part of the practitioner.

REFLECTION POINT

- *Consider the thoughts and feelings that the term personality disorder creates for you.*

Practitioners are people, and the feelings and ideas the term creates may be based on memories and attitudes that result in a negative view. Within a values framework the identification and addressing of beliefs is important.

Personality disorders and appropriate treatment

The definition of appropriate treatment under the amended Mental Health Act is that:

> ... *medical treatment must be appropriate, taking into account the nature and degree of the person's mental disorder and all their particular circumstances, including cultural, ethnic and religious considerations. By definition, it must be treatment which is for the purpose of alleviating or preventing a worsening of the patient's mental disorder or its symptoms or manifestations.*

(DoH 2008a; para 6.8)

For the purposes of the Act medical treatment includes nursing, psychological intervention and specialist mental health rehabilitation, habilitation and care (DoH, 2008a), and as such encompasses the full range of available psychosocial and biological interventions. As already indicated, what constitutes appropriate treatment is far from clear with this group of individuals, and as a result the local responses and availability of interventions can vary significantly.

The treatment of personality disorder has been subject to research by the National Institute of Clinical Excellence (NICE), and two guidance documents have been published, one documenting the recommended treatment for borderline personality disorder, and one recommended treatment for antisocial personality disorder (NCCMH, 2010; NCCMH, 2009). Both of these guidelines, along with the recommendations from the policy implementation guide (DoH, 2003b), state that inpatient acute psychiatric care is not recommended for individuals with personality disorder, and should only be utilised as a last resort during periods of significant risk. For the AMHP in practice this is a factor that should be considered: appropriate treatment can be applied to prevent the worsening of symptoms, and so admission to an acute unit can be used where the risk factors cannot be managed in another setting; however, there consideration must be given to whether the level of crisis the individual is presenting is sufficient, and whether the issue requires such a response for the health and safety of the individual or the protection of others.

CASE STUDY **10.3**

Isabelle is a 25-year-old single woman who lives alone in a rented flat in a town centre. She has been referred to mental health services a number of times over the last 8 years, and has repeatedly presented to the local A & E department following drug overdoses and self-injury. She is diagnosed as having borderline personality disorder. Over the last 2 years Isabelle has been accessing counselling support via a local women's centre and has been relatively stable, maintaining her tenancy and a part-time job as a secretary. Her mother has recently died and Isabelle's behaviour has become increasingly erratic: she has been drinking excessively and has not been going to work. Over the last month Isabelle has lost her job and has been arrested by the police for verbally abusing a man in the street. She has been going out in the evenings to clubs and behaving promiscuously. A referral is made by the police to the AMHP service, and Isabelle is detained under section 136 after being found in the town centre shouting at people in the street.

ACTIVITY **10.1**

- *As an AMHP assessing Isabelle, what are the appropriate treatment options available to her in your local area?*

Comment

Social and psychological treatments are recommended in the NICE guidance and policy guide, but will not immediately reduce the risks in Isabelle's case, and different services are available in different areas. The AMHP needs to be aware of what could be effective, and also whether it is available and accessible. Isabelle may require inpatient care or intensive community crisis input for a short period to minimise the current crisis, followed by psychosocial interventions to assist her to cope with her situation; this may include bereavement counselling, as this appears to be the trigger factor in this case.

Summary of key issues – personality disorder

Individuals diagnosed with personality disorder present with a range of complexities that AMHPs need to be aware of and consider in their assessment and decision-making processes. These include:

- Personality disorders can affect an individual's social situation, with difficulties in creating and maintaining relationships and an increased likelihood of risky behaviour, substance misuse and self-injury.

- Social difficulties are often experienced by individuals with a severe personality disorder – impulsivity and antisocial behaviour can lead to difficulties with housing, employment, and contact with the criminal justice system.

- The coexistence of a personality disorder and other mental health difficulty has a negative correlation with the success of any treatment intervention.

- Although mental health legislation now encompasses personality disorders within the definition of mental disorder, the assessment of appropriate treatment can be complex. The efficacy of treatments for personality disorder is a debated area, and it appears that social and psychological interventions have the greatest impact. The NICE guidelines for borderline and antisocial personality disorders both indicate that acute psychiatric inpatient care should only be a last resort when risk cannot be managed in any other way. As a result, AMHPs need to be aware of the facilities for this group in their local area, and have some knowledge as to what could be considered appropriate and under what circumstances.

- Stigma and prejudice are important considerations with this user group, who are largely viewed pessimistically by professionals. The AMHP should satisfy themselves that any decisions made regarding the availability of treatment and the appropriateness of services is based on an objective view of the individual's situation.

- Services vary greatly across the country, and individuals with personality disorders are often treated on the fringes of the mental health system. Local interpretation of the policy implementation guide for personality disorders is inconsistent, and AMHPs will need to have a full knowledge of local and out-of-area contracted services.

Conclusions

Substance misuse and personality disorders are just two groups of service users that the AMHP may encounter. These groups are often marginalised, with limited access to appropriate services and a history of risky behaviour and disengagement. Rates of social difficulty and risk of increased vulnerability are common, and such individuals are often excluded from their communities for various reasons. These types of difficulty can result in disillusionment with the system, and a lower likelihood of an appropriate response from services. Service availability and effectiveness are both aspects that an AMHP must be aware of to practise competently with these groups. As discussed, service availability varies, and to apply the least restrictive and effectiveness principles of the Act (DoH, 2008a) requires the practitioner to have an overview of what can be drawn upon to support an individual (and their family where relevant) as a alternative to admission and compulsion.

As a final consideration, it is often the case that a traumatic event or crisis is the trigger for presenting to services, and in many cases this will be the attention of the police or emergency services as a direct result of risk behaviour. This type of presentation further embeds the presumptions of both service users and workers, and the resulting negative expectations. AMHPs are often at the sharp end of this situation, being called out when a crisis has escalated to breaking point. The complexities and belief systems that exist in relation to these groups must be a consideration for the reflective practitioner, both as a requirement of their continuing professional development and also as evidence of considering the principles of the Act (DoH, 2008a) and ensuring anti-discriminatory practice is applied.

Chapter summary

- Coexisting conditions create an additional complexity to which services can struggle to respond.

- Certain service user groups become labelled by mental health professionals, and this leads to prejudice and presumptions.

- Practitioners need to be aware of the issues that affect complex groups and account for them in their assessments and decisions.

- Complex groups can create value conflicts in practitioners, and there is a need to examine and analyse personal reactions as part of ethical practice.

- Service users with multiple needs are at high risk of the full range of social and psychological problems, and services need to provide a holistic approach to assess and support these additional needs.

FURTHER READING

Department of Health (2002) *Mental Health Policy Implementation Guide Dual Diagnosis Good Practice Guide.* London: TSO.

Department of Health (2003) *Personality Disorder No Longer a Diagnosis of Exclusion – Policy Implementation Guidance for the Development of Services for People with Personality Disorder.* London: TSO.

Conclusion

Reasoning draws a conclusion, but does not make the conclusion certain, unless the mind discovers it by the path of experience.

Roger Bacon (c. 1214–1294), English philosopher and Franciscan friar

Introduction

Mental health practice involves a thorough understanding and consideration of power, prejudice and professional perspective, and the ethical dimension of this understanding is a vital element of competent practice.

A range of issues have been discussed, and the interrelation of human rights and ethical practice frameworks has been presented. This chapter will explore the issues presented throughout the book and attempt to bring together the key principles that influence ethical practice. The various frameworks and issues presented have enabled the exploration of a range of value considerations that are evident within mental health as a whole, and particularly in the AMHP and BIA roles.

The key objectives of this final chapter are to provide an understanding of the links between the various frameworks and dilemmas, and to encourage the reader to continue reflecting on their own actions and decisions as a key element in their continuing professional development.

A wide range of areas are linked to the development of values, including social, political, economic and psychological. Wider social values develop across time and circumstances, and what is considered ethical in one decade or one situation may not be so a decade later or in a different set of circumstances. Individual values are based on a whole host of factors, including wider social values, and as such need to be examined by the individual to assess the impact of them on their practice. The interaction of social and individual values can also create conflicts, and cultural experiences and understandings can differ across groups.

However, this is not an exhaustive representation. Throughout this book the importance of critical reflection has been highlighted as a cornerstone of ethical and value-based practice. Practitioners need to be able to step outside their practice to challenge their own and others' interventions where value judgements may be evident. This is not a comfortable thing to do, and competence in this area is a continual development need.

The social context of professional ethics

As with the development of the mental health value base, ethical considerations are also subject to social norms and expectations, and as such what is ethical has changed significantly throughout history. This book has presented two schools of ethical thought which are evident within mental health in an attempt to provide the reader with a framework and definition of what ethical practice means.

It is clear that mental health interventions have moved towards a system of self-determination, and the rights-based approach sits in the deontological tradition; however, other aspects of mental health intervention restrict this self-determination in the best interests of the individual or the public, and impinge upon individual rights as a result. This is a

Figure 11.1 Influences on value development

legal option and the Human Rights Act and European Convention on Human Rights both make allowances for actions that restrict the rights of individuals who are of 'unsound mind'; however, whether it is ethical depends on the approach subscribed to. Practitioners regularly balance these issues in their practice, and may need to make the transition across ethical schools as part of their decision making. This can be difficult and complex, but there is also a counter-argument that to do nothing could also be unethical, and such dilemmas are common.

The values of individual rights and best interests are what guide current professional decisions, and can help practitioners reconcile decisions with their professional ethics. Ethical practice ensures that even when restrictions are applied this is done with respect, participation, and the least amount of restriction necessary.

REFLECTION POINT

Deontological and teleological ethics are both applied to mental health in different situations.

- *In your opinion, in what circumstances do the ends justify the means (teleological) and in what circumstance are the means the most important ethical consideration (deontological)?*

Different practitioners will have different tolerances to risk and other behaviour, and the decision to apply interventions against an individual's wishes is influenced by these. The values, experience and competence of the practitioner all contribute to these types of decisions, and it is useful to reflect upon individual decisions to determine the rationale for action (or inaction) and what learning can be applied to develop future practice.

Values and social history

It is clear that values and ethics are essentially social constructions, and historically what is considered good practice has changed as a result of wider social and political contexts.

The history of both society and mental health treatment has had some dark moments, and those with mental health problems have been segregated, excluded and scapegoated at various times. The changes in social welfare during the 20th century and the reformist movement of the time, which promoted individual rights and society's duty to support those who were vulnerable, changed the mental health system beyond all recognition. This period provided the foundations for the contemporary system and drove some significant legislative reforms to improve both the system and the experience of those with mental health issues.

Although paternalistic values may still be evident within the system, the morality issues that were previously evident have largely been eradicated, and the understanding of what mental health conditions are and how they can be treated has advanced significantly.

Simon is 25 years old and experiencing an episode of psychosis. His behaviour has become increasingly erratic, and he has been found in public areas screaming and running up and down the street. Simon's mother and father are very distressed as they do not know what to do, and when staying with them recently he smashed all their crockery in a fit of anger.

Simon is a single man of Pakistani origin; he moved to the UK with his family when he was 2 years old and has not returned to Pakistan since. He is unemployed and has never worked, and is claiming incapacity benefit. He has a bedsit on an estate outside of town which is council owned, and claims housing benefit to pay his rent. Simon has been drinking on a daily basis and buys cheap cider from the off-licence, which he then drinks in the street. His behaviour becomes louder and more aggressive when he has been drinking, and the police have been called out once in the last week when he started shouting at a passer-by.

ACTIVITY **11.1**

- Considering the history of mental health treatment, what is the response that Simon would receive from services now compared to the early 20th century?
- What values are these differences based on?

Comment

In the current system Simon would be able to access community and short-stay inpatient support according to his needs. Services could also be offered to his family to help them maintain their support of Simon. Historically, Simon would have been considered in need of admission, and the welfare he receives would not have been available. The differences in support that Simon would receive at different periods in history is indicative of how mental health issues have been regarded, and although stigma and discrimination do still occur, the services available for Simon would uphold his rights and ensure that any institutional stay would be for the shortest time possible and only if his health and safety, or that of others, could not be managed in a community setting.

There are differences in local area responses that should be noted, and whereas some areas have a progressive approach others are slower to embrace the wider social approaches.

Values and social context

Social values are complex and can be difficult to define; however, the overall approach to mental health issues has begun to shift in alignment with how society views individuals who are vulnerable or have particular needs. Social, economic and political views all affect social responses, and the move towards a welfare-based approach that followed the second world war resulted in a system of socialised medicine and local authority responsibility that was accessible by all, regardless of class or the ability to pay. As society has developed and treatments progressed, the social response to mental health has become more accepting. Since the mid-20th century there has been an explicit acknowledgement that mental illness can be treated or managed, and the duty placed on society to provide such treatment is a direct reflection of social values and the rights-based approach. Despite these developments there remains a significant negative attitude towards mental health in some sectors of society, and this must be acknowledged and continue to be challenged.

At times in history there has been an emphasis on perceived morality which has affected those experiencing mental distress. Religious following and the social power of the Church has at times dictated what is socially acceptable, and although this is now less the case the impact of culture and belief on the experience of and response to mental health issues remains a consideration.

The developments in understanding of mental health and the emergence of the disability rights movement have introduced a range of approaches, most notably the social model and recovery approaches, which recognise the individual's strengths and the impact of the social context on well-being. These models are a significant step forward in terms of the user's experience of service delivery, as they approach the person in holistic terms and are focused on the principles of self-determination and personal dignity, both elements which are proven to improve recovery and overall outcome.

Cultural aspects of an individual's experience remain a significant consideration for practitioners, and the developments in the equality and diversity agendas support the self-determination and rights-based approaches. Culture affects us all: our attitudes, beliefs and behaviours are shaped by the culture we are part of and roles that we play. This can include family structures, spirituality, and customs and practices that all shape how we as individuals understand and interact with our environments. This recognition of culture as an important influence on individual and community well-being is another development that has progressed in more recent years, and is representative of the multicultural society in which we live.

The evidence that has emerged over the last 20 years has indicated that outcomes are improved for people when they are socially included, and this has been a significant focus of service delivery, with aspects such as occupation and employment support, welfare advice and social skills training all becoming part of service delivery options. While there remains a high degree of stigma associated with mental health conditions this is a difficult aim to achieve, and practitioners are required to challenge stigma and prejudice as part of their practice. Personal values are an important consideration in this area, with practitioners being required to work in accordance with service user values. These can at times conflict with their value base, and reflection and quality supervision are needed to maintain these skills.

Issues such as class, education, social network and employment can all affect an individual's experience of both mental health issues and the treatment system, and it is clear that social issues are still very much linked to mental health services. Poverty, family break-down, crime and substance misuse are all prevalent in the mental health population, and inequalities in physical health and well-being remain evident. Access to universal services, such as primary health and leisure facilities, are still affected by negative views of mental health, and challenge is needed across the whole public service system to address this. Social context can have a significant impact on an individual's health and well-being, and although treatment advances reflect this understanding there remains a role for practitioners in facilitating access, challenging inequality and supporting individual rights.

The pervading social values in England and Wales are based on principles of individual rights and public protection, and in some situations these can be difficult to reconcile. Disparities in power between workers and service users has been a traditional feature of mental health services, and although formal measures remain an option these are now carried out with a view to respect for the individual and their participation wherever possible.

CASE STUDY 11.2

Stuart is a 43-year-old man who is homeless and a street drinker. He has been in mental health services for 20 years and has had regular admissions to the local inpatient unit. Stuart has sporadic contact with the community mental health team and his psychiatrist, usually at times of crisis.

Stuart has been excluded from his GP practice as he can become very agitated and frighten other patients; however, he has no history of violence. Stuart's physical health is poor and he has a persistent cough, and the chemist will not sell him cough medicine as they think he is misusing it.

He has a criminal record for acquisitive crime – mainly shop theft – and has a significant amount of debt. He is currently staying at the local night shelter, as he was evicted from his last accommodation for rent arrears, and the council will not offer him a further flat until he has cleared these debts.

ACTIVITY 11.2

- What elements of Stuart's social context are likely to contribute to his mental health issues and overall well-being?

- What actions would you suggest to address these issues?

Stuart's situation is not uncommon, and although mental health services may try and provide treatment, the social issues that Stuart is experiencing are likely to make interventions less effective. Engagement with Stuart should be the priority, with issues such as trust and rapport being addressed via partnership in the assessment and care planning processes. Stuart would benefit from help to access welfare supports such as benefits advice, and help to talk to the council about his housing arrears; in addition, some primary care services are needed for his physical health and a GP needs to be identified. In this situation it would be more effective to help Stuart with his social issues than to offer him structured treatment based on the values of social inclusion and integration.

Values and policy

As social values have changed so too have the guiding policies that services operate within, and there is now a central focus on empowerment and promoting individual rights. The national service framework (DoH, 1998) set out an ambitious plan to modernise mental health services, and over its lifespan increased community-based services and less reliance on containment in inpatient facilities have been achieved. The popularity of the recovery approach has further developed how services are delivered, and the integration of health and social care has improved accessibility and created a wider range of support options.

The emphasis on social inclusion has required cooperation between community and public services, with employers, educational establishments and other service providers required to engage with the agenda. Equality legislation and duties have strengthened this requirement, and mental health is now an area that the whole of society needs to support.

The *New Horizons* mental health strategy emphasises the need for social system support and social inclusion measures such as activity, employment and social interactions, to be an integral part of the mental health system, and this is consistent with the drive towards addressing social inequality.

Policy is reflective of social values, and in a western society that values difference and the individual contributions of citizens, policy has needed significant development and modernisation to ensure that social and community priorities are represented in how services respond to vulnerable members of society.

REFLECTION POINT

- *What do you feel are the most important aspects of the* New Horizons *strategy key themes?*

- *How do these relate to the social values and context?*

The themes of *New Horizons* are based on personalisation, recovery, prevention and equality, all prevalent factors in other areas of public service. The drive towards service user choice and control is consistent with the overall climate of human rights and social inclusion, which have both been shown to improve outcomes for both individuals and communities.

Values and legislation

Like policy direction, legislation must reflect public opinion and attitudes, and mental health law has undergone a dramatic transformation over the last century. At the beginning of this period power belonged with the professions and mental health issues were viewed as needing containment. The emphasis on inpatient treatment was developed alongside the widespread use of large asylums, and psychiatry viewed institutionalisation as the most effective treatment option. As social models have been introduced and an evidence base discovered this has changed, and the reform of the welfare system has spurred on these developments.

In contemporary care systems community interventions and localisation are considered the most effective treatment option, with inpatient admission only considered where there are no other alternatives available to manage the risk. Although the professionals have retained the power to make these decisions, there are core values and criteria that must be evident for these sanctions to be lawful, with options for redress and challenge for the individual. In this situation, although criticism can still be levelled at services which are seen as paternalistic and risk averse, there are mechanisms and safeguards in place and the power is no longer absolute as it once was.

The Mental Health Act 1983 (as amended) and the Mental Capacity Act 2005 strike a balance between individual rights and protection, and are explicit in the expectations placed on practitioners. This represents significant progress when viewed in the historical context of mental health legislation and treatment.

Assessment processes need to evidence the guiding principles of the relevant Code of Practice, and it is useful for practitioners to reflect on how they apply the principles in their decision making. During the assessment itself the judgements may not be as explicit, with pressures and circumstances dictating particular responses; however, this is not the end of the process for the practitioner, and at the report-writing stage it can be useful to identify the decisions and interventions that were made and how they relate to the principles.

The Codes of Practice that guide statutory decision making are essentially value based, with clear principles that reflect the modern view of mental illness and individual rights. These are the bibles that should guide mental health practice, and are strengthened by the informal treatment system, which is developing further to become user-directed and based on a relationship between user and service provider. The decisions that practitioners are required to make are complex and have significant ramifications for the individual. This is a significant amount of power invested in individual practitioners, and as such a clear ethical framework which sets out the value base for actions ensures that practitioners are operating from a consistent basis.

Over recent years there has been an emphasis on equality and diversity which is reflective of the multicultural society England and Wales have become. As economic migration has increased so too has the range of cultures, customs and traditions among the population. Anti-discriminatory practice is an area that is well developed, and recent legal developments have also enshrined it within the statutory framework. Human rights have become the common framework across public services, and organisations have specific duties to address discrimination across the six equality strands.

In mental health terms there is a dual impact of equality and diversity issues: first, in marginalised populations individuals are likely to experience exclusion, access issues and isolation, all of which indicate a higher risk of mental health issues. Second, services need to respond to and understand the particular needs resulting from the individual's culture to avoid compounding any difficulties. This is a situation that has yet to be resolved, and both over-representation and under-representation of certain groups is still evident in mental health care.

It should be noted that culture in this context does not relate exclusively to race, religion or ethnic origin, but applies across the whole range of equality strands and has particular impact on individuals with multiple identities, for example a Polish lesbian woman who is a mother will have specific cultural needs relating to each of these identities.

REFLECTION POINT

- *How do you consider and evidence your application of the Mental Health Act or Mental Capacity Act guiding principles within your practice?*

- *How were these met or not met by services?*

Cultural needs is a wide category and can include a range of issues such as diet, dress, religious ceremony, interaction with the opposite gender, physical access to premises and particular treatment methods. Each individual needs to be assessed in their own context to identify any adjustments or particular facilities they may need to maintain their cultural context. It also needs to be recognised that all needs will not be met by all services, and there will be times when specialist facilities or supports will be necessary. Practitioners will therefore need to apply culturally competent practice and be aware of the range of appropriate treatment options available.

As discussed throughout this book, values are subjective and influenced by a range of social and psychological factors; the guiding principles of the Codes of Practice are the vehicle that ensures that a holistic and rights-based view of the individual is applied, and decisions are not unduly affected by individual confidence, knowledge or attitudes. Values are not only the guiding principles, but also include the practitioner reflecting on their personal views, attitudes and beliefs and considering how they influence their decision making. This approach is embedded in social work, and as the new roles have been established, as well as a shared vision, it has also become a requirement of all professionals within the delivery of value based mental health practice.

Conclusion

The values and ethics of mental health practice is a diverse and complex topic and the impact of social and individual values compounds this. This chapter has attempted to provide an overview of some of the issues in relation to value based practice that have been highlighted throughout this book, as an indication of how values underpin the strategy and delivery of mental health care.

Social welfare ideals are the foundations of the mental health system, and progresses in societal attitude have transformed this system from a punitive and judgemental approach to one based on the principles of human rights and self-determination. As discussed, practitioners in the field have a difficult balance to strike between protection and empowerment, and many aspects affect how they approach and intervene in an individual's life.

This book does not seek to provide answers, for that would be impossible, but rather highlights a range of issues that face mental health practitioners and provides the opportunity for learning and reflection within a sound theoretical and practice-based framework.

The dynamic nature of values and ethics is subject to a multitude of individual and social forces, and so the development of value based practice will forever be subject to change in accordance with the social context.

Summary

- Values and ethics occur in the context of social history and are based on the pervading norms and expectations of society, and so what is considered ethical changes over time.

- Ethical theories are in place within mental health, but there are two different approaches which are applied according to circumstances.

- Individual rights and dignity are key principles of all mental health care and practitioners need to develop the skills to balance these with the protective measures used.

- Policy and legislation reflect the wider social values and create a framework for practice to guide decisions and interventions.

FURTHER READING

Bloch, S and Green, SA (2009) (4th Ed) *Psychiatric Ethics*. Oxford: Oxford University Press.

Gilbert, P (2003) *The Value of Everything: Social Work and Its Importance in the Field of Mental Health*. Lyme Regis: Russell House.

References

Alaszewski, A (2002) Risk and dangerousness, in Bytheway, B, Bacigalupo, V, Bornat, J et al. (eds), *Understanding Care, Welfare and Community: A Reader*. London: Routledge, 183–191.

Alcock, P (1996) *Social Policy in Britain: Themes and Issues*. Basingstoke: Macmillan.

Aldridge, J and Becker, S (1993) *Children Caring for Parents with Mental Illness: Perspectives of Young People, Parents and Professionals*. Bristol: Polity Press.

American Psychiatric Association (1994) *Diagnostic and Statistical Manual of Mental Disorders (DSM VI)*. Arlington VA: AMA.

Andrews, J, Briggs, A, Porter, R and Tucker, P (1997) *The History of Bethlem Hospital*. London: Routledge.

Angermeyer, MC and Matschinger, H (2004) The stereotype of schizophrenia and its impact on discrimination against people with schizophrenia: Results from a representative survey in Germany. *Schizophrenia Bulletin*, 30 (4), 1049–1061.

Anthony, WA (1993) Recovery from mental illness: The guiding vision of the mental health service system in the 1990s. *Psychosocial Rehabilitation Journal*, 16 (4), 11–23.

Appleby, L (2000) A new mental health service: High quality and user-led. *British Journal of Psychiatry*, 177, 290–291.

Banerjee, S, Clancy, C and Crome, I (2002) *Coexisting Problems of Mental Disorder and Substance Misuse (Dual Diagnosis)*. London: Royal College of Psychiatrists.

Banks, S (2006) *Ethics and Values in Social Work,* 3rd edition. Basingstoke: Palgrave Macmillan.

Barber, P, Brown, R and Martin, D (2009) *Mental Health Law in England and Wales*. Exeter: Learning Matters.

Barnard, A (2008) Values, ethics and professionalization: A social work history, in Barnard, A, Horner, N, and Wild, J (eds) *Value Base of Social Work and Social Care: An Active Learning Handbook*. Maidenhead: Open University Press.

Barnes, M, Bowl, R and Fisher, M (1990) *Sectioned: Social Services and the 1983 Mental Health Act*. London: Routledge.

Bartlett, P (1999) *The Poor Law of Lunacy*. Leicester: Leicester University Press.

Bastide, R (1972) *Sociology of Mental Disorder* (translated by J McNeil). Abingdon: Routledge and Kegan Paul.

Bateman, AW and Fonagy, P (2000) Effectiveness of psychotherapeutic treatment of personality disorders. *British Journal of Psychiatry*, 177, 138–143.

Battie, W (1758) *The Treatise of Madness*. Classics of Psychiatry and Behavioral Sciences Library [out of print].

Bayer, T, Tadd, W and Krajcik, S (2005) Dignity: The voice of older people. Quality in ageing. *Policy Practice and Research*, 6, 22–29.

BBC (1999) *The Origins of Community Care* [online]. Available at: http://news.bbc.co.uk/1/hi/health/229517.stm

Beach, SR, Schulz, R, Williamson, GM et al. (2005) Risk factors for potentially harmful informal caregiver behaviour. *Journal of the American Geriatrics Society*, 53, 255–261.

Beck, U (1992) *Risk Society: Towards a New Modernity*. London: Sage.

Beigel, A and Santiago, JM (1995) Redefining the general psychiatrist: Values, reforms and issues for psychiatric residency education. *Psychiatric Services*, 46, 769–774.

Beresford, P (2006) User involvement, research and health inequalities: Developing new directions. *Health and Social Care in the Community*, 15 (4), 306–312.

Bichard, Sir M (2004) *The Bichard Inquiry Report*. London: HMSO.

Bisman, C (2003) Social work values: The moral core of the profession. *British Journal of Social Work*, 34 (1), 9–123.

Bloch, S and Green, SA (2006) An ethical framework for psychiatry. *British Journal of Psychiatry*, 188, 7–12.

Bloch, S and Green, SA (2009) *Psychiatric Ethics*, 4th edition. Oxford: Oxford University Press.

Blofeld, J, Sallah, D, Sashidharan, S and Struthers, J (2003) *Independent Inquiry into the Death of David Bennett*. Cambridge: Norfolk, Suffolk, and Cambridge Strategic Health Authority.

BMA (2006) *Parliamentary Brief: Mental Health Bill, House of Lords, Second Reading – 28 November 2006*. Available at: www.mentalhealthalliance.org.uk/policy/documents/BMA_Bill_Lords_2R_Briefing.pdf

Boehnlein, JK (2000) *Psychiatry and Religion: The Convergence of Mind and Spirit (Issues in Psychiatry)*. Arlington, VA: American Psychiatric Press.

Bogg, D (2008) *The Integration of Mental Health Social Work and the NHS*. Exeter: Learning Matters.

Bowers, L and Allen, T (2006) The Attitude to Personality Disorder Questionnaire: Psychometric properties and results. *Journal of Personality Disorders*, 20 (3), 281–293.

Brandon, D, Brandon, A and Brandon, T (1995) *Advocacy: Power to People with Disabilities*. Birmingham: Venture.

Braveman, P and Gruskin, S (2003) Defining equity in health. *Journal of Epidemiological Community Health*, 27, 254–258.

Bray, I, Waraich, P, Jones, W et al. (2006) Increase in schizophrenia incidence rates: Findings in a Canadian cohort born 1975–1985. *Social Psychiatry and Psychiatric Epidemiology*, 41, 611–618.

Breeze, J (1998) Can paternalism be justified in mental health care? *Journal of Advanced Nursing*, 28 (2), 260–265.

Bridge, C and Bridge, G (1984) Civil commitment: A multi-disciplinary analysis. *Law Review*, 14 (2), 145–157.

Brimblecombe, N (2006) Asylum nursing as a career in the United Kingdom, 1890–1910. *Journal of Advanced Nursing*, 55 (6), 770–777.

British Association of Social Work (2002) *Code of Ethics for Social Work.* Birmingham: BASW. Available at: www.basw.co.uk/about/codeofethics/

British Psychological Society (2009) *Code of Ethics and Conduct.* London: British Psychological Society.

Brunette, MF and Dean, W (2002) Community mental health care for woman with severe mental illness who are parents. *Community Mental Health Journal*, 38 (2), 153–165.

Byrne, P (2001) Psychiatric stigma. *British Journal of Psychiatry*, 178, 281–284.

Campbell, D and McLean, C (2002) Ethnic identities, social capital and health inequalities: Factors shaping African Caribbean participation in local community networks in the UK. *Social Science and Medicine*, 55 (4), 643–657.

Cantor-Graae, E and Selten, JP (2005) Schizophrenia and migration: A meta-analysis and review. *American Journal of Psychiatry*, 162, 12–24.

Capitman, J (2002) Defining diversity: A primer and a review. *Generations*, 26 (3), 8–14.

Care Quality Commission (2009) *A New System of Registration: Guide for Providers of Healthcare or Adult Social Care.* London: Care Quality Commission.

Carlson, ET (1973) The death of the asylum. *Bulletin of the New York Academy of Medicine*, 50 (5), 636–649.

Carpenter, J (2002) Mental health recovery paradigm: Implications for social work. *Health and Social Work*, 27 (2), 86–94.

Cass, E, Robins, D and Richardson, A (2009) *Dignity in Care: SCIE Guide 15.* London: SCIE.

Chaloner, C (1999) Ethics and morality, in Chaloner, C and Coffrey, M (eds) *Forensic Mental Health Nursing.* Chichester: Wiley.

Chamberlin, J (1990) The ex-patients' movement: Where we've been and where we're going. *Journal of Mind and Behaviour*, 11 (3–4), 323–336.

Chief Nursing Officer (2006) *From Values to Action: The Chief Nursing Officer's Review of Mental Health Nursing.* London: TSO.

Chief Nursing Officer (2007) *Privacy and Dignity – A Report by the Chief Nursing Officer into Mixed Sex Accommodation in Hospitals.* London: TSO.

Chief Secretary to the Treasury (2003) *Every Child Matters.* Cm5860. London: HMSO.

Chochinov, HM, Hack, T, Hassard, T et al. (2005) Dignity therapy: A novel psychotherapeutic intervention for patients near the end of life. *Journal of Clinical Oncology*, 23 (24), 5520–5525.

Cleary, M (2003) The challenges of mental health care reform for contemporary mental health nursing practice: Relationships, power and control. *International Journal of Mental Health Nursing*, 12, 139–147.

Cohen, S (1985) *Visions of Social Control: Crime, Punishment and Classification.* Bristol: Polity Press.

Coleborn, C (2001) Exhibiting madness: Material culture and the asylum. *Health and History*, 3 (2), 104–117.

College of Occupational Therapy (2005) *Code of Ethics and Professional Conduct.* London: COT.

College of Occupational Therapy (2008) *The Value of Occupational Therapy and Its Contribution to Adult Social Service Users and Their Carers.* Position Statement. Available at: www.cot.org.uk/MainWebSite/Resources/Document/The%20value%20of%20OT%20and%20its%20contribution.pdf

Cook, JA and Jonikas, JA (2002) Self-determination among mental health consumers/survivors. *Journal of Disability Policy Studies*, 13 (2), 88–96.

Copeland, ME (2004) Self-determination in mental health recovery: Taking back our lives, in Jonikas, J and Cook, J (eds) *UIC NRTC's National Self-Determination and Psychiatric Disability.* Invitational Conference: Conference Papers 68–82. Chicago, IL: UIC National Research and Training Center on Psychiatric Disability.

Corrigan, P (2004) How stigma interferes with mental health care. *American Psychologist*, 59 (7), 614–625.

Corrigan, P (2007) How clinical diagnosis might exacerbate the stigma of mental illness. *Social Work*, 52 (1), 31–39.

Corrigan, P and Watson A (2002) Understanding the impact of stigma on people with mental illness. *World Psychiatry*, 1 (1), 16–20.

Cottone, RR (2001) A social constructivism model of ethical decision making in counselling. *Journal of Counselling and Development*, 79 (1), 39–45.

Crossley, N (2006) *Contesting Psychiatry: Social Movements in Mental Health.* Abingdon: Routledge.

CSIP (2006) *Direct Payments For People With Mental Health Problems: A Guide to Action.* London: DoH.

CSIP/NIMHE (2006) *The Social Work Contribution to Mental Health Services: The Future Direction.* Report of responses to the discussion paper. Available at: www.scie.org.uk/publications/consultation/contribution-final.pdf

Curran, C, Burxgardt, T, Knapp, M et al. (2007) Challenges in multidisciplinary systematic reviewing: A study on social exclusion and mental health policy. *Social Policy and Administration*, 41 (3), 289–312.

Dakin, M (2007) *Whose Secret? Protecting Vulnerable Adults from Abuse.* Solihull Metropolitan Borough Council. London: Pavilion.

Dalrymple, J and Burke, B (1995) *Anti-Oppressive Practice: Social Care and the Law.* Buckingham: Open University Press.

Darzi, Lord (2008) *High Quality Care for All: The Final Report of the NHS Next Stage Review.* London: TSO.

Deci, EL and Ryan, RM (2002) An overview of self-determination theory: An organismic-dialectical perspective, in Deci, EL and Ryan, RM (eds) *Handbook of Self-Determination Research.* Rochester, NY: University of Rochester Press.

Deegan P (1996) Recovery as a journey of the heart. *Psychiatric Rehabilitation Journal*, 19 (3), 91–97.

Dein, K, Williams, PS and Dein, S (2007) Ethnic bias in the application of the Mental Health Act 1983. *Advances in Psychiatric Treatment*, 13, 350–357.

Department of Children, Schools and Families (2006) *Working Together to Safeguard Children.* London: DCSF.

Department of Children, Schools and Families (2007) *The Children's Plan: Building Brighter Futures.* London: DCSF.

Department of Children, Schools and Families (2008) *Think Family Toolkit: Improving Support for Families at Risk – Strategic Overview.* London: TSO.

Department of Children, Schools and Families (2010) *Working Together to Safeguard Children.* London: DCSF.

Department of Constitutional Affairs (2007) *Mental Capacity Act 2005 Code of Practice.* London: TSO.

Department of Constitutional Affairs (2008) *Deprivation of Liberty Safeguards: Code of Practice to Supplement the Main Mental Capacity Act 2005 Code of Practice.* London: TSO.

Department of Health (1998) *Modernising Mental Health Services: Safe, Sound and Supportive.* London: TSO.

Department of Health (1999a) *National Service Framework for Mental Health.* London: TSO.

Department of Health (1999b) *Reform of the Mental Health Act 1983: Proposals for Consultation.* London: TSO.

Department of Health (2000) *No Secrets: Guidance on Developing and Implementing Multi-Agency Policies and Procedures to Protect Vulnerable Adults from Abuse.* London: TSO.

Department of Health (2001) *Reforming the Mental Health Act.* London: TSO.

Department of Health (2002) *Mental Health Policy Implementation Guide: Dual Diagnosis Good Practice Guide.* London: TSO.

Department of Health (2003a) *National Occupational Standards for Mental Health: Implementation Guide.* London: TSO.

Department of Health (2003b) *Personality Disorder: No Longer a Diagnosis of Exclusion – Policy Implementation Guidance for the Development of Services for People with Personality Disorder.* London: TSO.

Department of Health (2005a) *Delivering Race Equality in Mental Health Care: An Action Plan for Reform Inside and Outside of Services and the Government's Response to the Independent Inquiry into the Death of David Bennett.* London: TSO.

Department of Health (2005b) *Bournewood Consultation: The Approach to be Taken in Response to the Judgment of the European Court of Human Rights in the Bournewood Case.* London: TSO.

Department of Health (2006a) *Next Steps for the Mental Health Bill.* Press Release 23/03/06. Available at: www.dh.gov.uk/en/Publicationsandstatistics/Pressreleases/DH_4132068

Department of Health (2006b) *Our Health, Our Care, Our Say: A New Direction For Community Services.* London: TSO.

Department of Health (2006c) *Dual Diagnosis in Mental Health Inpatient and Day Hospital Settings: Guidance on the Assessment and Management of Patients in Mental Health Inpatient and Day Hospital Settings Who Have Mental Ill-Health and Substance Use Problems.* London: TSO.

Department of Health (2007a) *New Ways of Working for Everyone.* London: TSO.

Department of Health (2007b) *Capabilities for Inclusive Practice.* London: TSO.

Department of Health (2007c) *Putting People First: A Shared Vision and Commitment to the Transformation of Adult Social Care.* London: TSO.

Department of Health (2007d) *Independence Choice and Risk.* London: TSO.

Department of Health (2007e) *Best Practice in Managing Risk: Principles and Guidance for Best Practice in the Assessment and Management of Risk to Self and Others in Mental Health Services.* London: TSO.

Department of Health (2008a) *Mental Health Act 1983 Code of Practice.* London: TSO.

Department of Health (2008b) *A High Quality Workforce: NHS Next Stage Review.* London: TSO.

Department of Health (2008c) *LAC (2008)1: Transforming Adult Social Care.* Available at: www.dh.gov.uk/en/Publicationsandstatistics/Lettersandcirculars/LocalAuthorityCirculars/DH_081934

Department of Health (2008d) *Dignity in Care: Becoming a Champion.* London: TSO.

Department of Health (2008e) S*afeguarding Adults: A Consultation on the Review of the 'No Secrets' Guidance.* London: TSO.

Department of Health (2008f) *Carers at the Heart of 21st Century Families and Communities: A Caring System On Your Side, A Life of Your Own.* London: TSO.

Department of Health (2008g) *What are the Mental Capacity Act 2005 Deprivation of Liberty Safeguards?* Information leaflet produced by COI on behalf of the Department of Health, Gateway No.10989. London: TSO.

Department of Health (2009a) *New Horizons: Working Together for Better Mental Health.* London: TSO.

Department of Health (2009b) *The Operating Framework for the NHS in England 2009/10: High Quality Care for All.* London: TSO.

Department of Health (2009c) *The NHS Constitution: A Consultation on New Patient Rights.* London: TSO.

Department of Health (2009d) *Shaping the Future of Care Together.* London: TSO.

Department of Health (2009e) *Working to Put People First: The Strategy for the Adult Social Care Workforce in England.* London: TSO.

Department of Health (2009f) *Safeguarding Adults: Report on the Consultation on the Review of 'No Secrets'.* London: TSO.

Department of Health (2010) Equity and Excellence: *Liberating the NHS.* London: TSO.

Department of Health (2010) *Written Ministerial Statement. Government Response to the Consultation on Safeguarding Adults of the 'No Secrets' Guidance.* Tuesday 19 January 2010. Available at: www.dh.gov.uk/en/Consultations/Responsestoconsultations/DH_111286

Department of Health Expert Committee (1999) *Review of the Mental Health Act 1983: Report of the Expert Committee.* London: DH.

Dinos, S, Stevens, S, Serfaty, M et al. (2004) Stigma: The feelings and experiences of 46 people with mental illness. *British Journal of Psychiatry*, 184, 176–181.

Double, D (2006) *Critical Psychiatry: The Limits of Madness.* Basingstoke: Palgrave Macmillan.

Douglas, M (1994) *Risk and Blame: Essays in Cultural Theory.* London: Routledge.

Driver, F (1993) *Power and Pauperism: The Workhouse System 1834–1884.* Cambridge: Cambridge University Press.

Duggan, M, Cooper, A and Foster, J (2002) *Modernising the Social Model in Mental Health: A Discussion Paper.* London: SPN.

Fennell, P (2008) Best interests and treatment for mental disorder. *Health Care Analysis*, 16, 255–267.

Floyd Taylor, M (2006) Is self-determination still important? What experienced mental health social workers are saying. *Journal of Social Work Values and Ethics*, 3 (1) [online]. Available at: www.socialworker.com/jswve/content/view/29/44/

Foucault, M (1982) Afterword: The subject and power, in Foucault, M *Beyond Structuralism and Hermeneutics*, 2nd edition (eds H.L. Dreyfus and P. Rabinow). Brighton: Harvester Press.

Foucault, M (1991) Governmentality, in Buchell, G, Gordon, C and Miller, P (eds) *The Foucault Effect: Studies in Governmentality.* Hemel Hempstead: Harvester Wheatsheaf.

Freud, S (1965) *The Origin and Development of Psychoanalysis.* Michigan, USA: Regnery Gateway [out of print].

Garno, JL, Goldberg, JF, Ramirez, PM and Ritzler, BA (2005) Bipolar disorder with comorbid cluster B personality disorder features: Impact on suicidality. *Journal of Clinical Psychiatry*, 66 (3), 339–345.

Gasper, D (2004) *Human Well-Being: Concepts and Conceptualizations.* United Nations University WIDER, Discussion Paper No. 2004/06. Available at: www.wider.unu.edu/stc/repec/pdfs/rp2004/dp2004–06.pdf

Gibbins, J (1988) Residential care for mentally ill adults, in Sinclair, I (ed) *Residential Care: The Research Reviewed.* London: HMSO.

Gigerenzer, E (2003) *Reckoning with Risk: Learning to Live with Uncertainty.* Harmondsworth: Penguin.

Gilbert, P (2003) *The Value of Everything: Social Work and Its Importance in the Field of Mental Health.* Lyme Regis: Russell House.

Gilburt, H, Rose, D and Slade, M (2008) The importance of relationship in mental health care: A qualitative study of service users' experiences of psychiatric hospital admission in the UK. *BMC Health Services Research*, 8, 92 [online]. Available at: www.biomedcentral.com/1472–6963/8/92

Glasby, J and Beresford, P (2006) Evidence-based practice and the service user contribution. *Critical Social Policy*, 26 (1), 268–284.

Glover, G and Evison, F (2009) *Use of Mental Health Services by Ethnic Minorities in England.* Stockton on Tees: North East Public Health Observatory.

Gorczynska, T (2007) The first legal right to advocacy. *Working with Older People*, 11 (1), 17–20.

Grafstrom, M, Nordberg, A and Winblad, B (1993) Abuse is in the eye of the beholder. *Scandinavian Journal of Public Health*, 21 (4), 247–255.

Griffin-Heslin, VL (2005) An analysis of the concept dignity. *Accident and Emergency Nursing*, 13, 251–257.

Griffiths, L (2001) Categorising to exclude: The discursive construction of cases in community mental health teams. *Sociology of Health and Illness*, 23 (5), 678–700.

Guardian (1999) What is institutional racism? Wednesday 24 February 1999. Available at: www.guardian.co.uk/uk/1999/feb/24/lawrence.ukcrime7

Hare R (1993) *The Philosophical Basis of Psychiatric Ethics*. New York: Oxford University Press.

Haringey LSCB (2009) *Serious Case Review: Baby Peter*. Executive Summary. Available at: www.haringeylscb.org/executive_summary_peter_final.pdf

HL v United Kingdom (Bournewood) 45508/99 (2004) ECHR 471.

Hope, R (2004) *The Ten Essential Shared Capabilities – A Framework for the Whole of the Mental Health Workforce*. London: TSO.

Hopkins, E (1979) *A Social History of the English Working Classes 1815–1945*. London: Hodder & Stoughton.

Hopton, J (2006) The future of critical psychiatry. *Critical Social Policy*, 26 (1), 57–73.

Howe, Earl (2009) *Same-Sex Accommodation in Hospitals: Why It Matters and Progress on Implementing Policy*. Report of a Cross Parliamentary Panel. Available at: www.institute.nhs.uk/images//documents/DSSA/MIXED%20FINAL%20Earl%20Howe%20report%20on%20same-sex%20accommodation.pdf

Hudson, CG (2005) Socioeconomic status and mental illness: Tests of social causation and selection hypotheses. *American Journal of Orthopsychiatry*, 75 (1), 3–18.

Hugo, M (2001) Mental health professionals' views of people who have experienced mental health problems. *Journal of Psychiatric and Mental Health Nursing*, 8 (5), 419–425.

Hui, A and Stickley, T (2007) Mental health policy and mental health service user perspectives on involvement: A discourse analysis. *Journal of Advanced Nursing*, 59 (4), 416–426.

Independent Police Complaints Commission (2008) *Police Custody as a 'Place of Safety': Examining the Use of Section 136 of the Mental Health Act 1983*. IPCC research and statistic series: Paper 11.

International Federation of Social Work (2004) *Ethics in Social Work, Statement of Principles* [online]. Available at: www.ifsw.org/p38000324.html

Jacelon, CS, Connelly, TW, Brown, R et al. (2004) A concept analysis of dignity for older adults. *Journal of Advanced Nursing*, 48, 76–83.

Jacobson, N and Curtis, L (2000) Recovery as policy in mental health services: Strategies emerging from the States. *Psychiatric Rehabilitation Journal*, 23 (4), 333–341.

Jain, S (2003) Psychiatry and confinement in India, in Porter, R and Wright, D (eds) *The Confinement of the Insane: International Perspectives 1800–1965*. Cambridge: Cambridge University Press.

James, S and Prilleltensky, I (2002) Cultural diversity and mental health: Towards integrative practice. *Clinical Psychology Review*, 22 (8), 1133–1154.

JE v DE and Surrey County Council (2006) EWHC 3459 (Fam).

Jenkins, CJ (1983) Resource mobilization theory and the study of social movements. *Annual Review of Sociology*, 9, 527–553.

Jenkins, R (1992) *Pierre Bourdieu.* London: Routledge.

Joint Committee on the Draft Mental Health Bill (2005) *First Report.* London: TSO.

Joint Committee on Human Rights (2002) *Draft Mental Health Bill: Twenty-Fifth Report of Sessions 2001–2.* London: TSO.

Joint Committee on Human Rights (2008) *Legislative Scrutiny: Health and Social Care Bill, Seventh Report of Sessions 2007–8.* London: TSO.

Jones, K (1960) *Mental Health and Social Policy, 1845–1959.* London: Routledge.

Jones, R (2008) *Mental Capacity Act Manual*, 3rd edition. London: Sweet & Maxwell.

Jones, R (2009) *Mental Health Act Manual*, 12th edition. London: Sweet & Maxwell.

Kahneman, D and Tversky, A (2000) *Choices, Values and Frames.* Cambridge: Cambridge University Press.

Keating, F, Robertson, D and Kotecha, N (2003) *Ethnic Diversity and Mental Health in London: Recent Developments.* London: Kings Fund.

Kendell, S (2001) The distinction between mental and physical illness. *British Journal of Psychiatry*, 178, 490–493.

Kerkorian, D, McKay, M, Bannon, JR and William, M (2006) Seeking help a second time: Parents'/caregivers' characterizations of previous experiences with mental health services for their children and perceptions of barriers to future use. *American Journal of Orthopsychiatry*, 76 (2), 161–166.

Kernberg, OF and Michels, R (2009) Editorial – borderline personality disorder. *American Journal of Psychiatry*, 166 (5), 505–508.

Kesey, K (1962) *One Flew Over the Cuckoo's Nest.* New York: Signet.

Kirkbride, JB, Fearon, P, Morgan, C et al. (2006) Heterogeneity in incidence rates of schizophrenia and other psychotic syndromes – findings from the 3-center ÆSOP study. *Archives of General Psychiatry*, 63, 250–258.

Kmietowicz, Z (2002) New mental health bill may conflict with advice from the GMC. *British Medical Journal*, 325, 678.

Koenig, HG (2005) *Faith and Mental Health: Religious Resources for Healing.* West Conshohocken, PA: Templeton Press.

Kraepelin, E (1906) *Lectures in Clinical Psychiatry.* Authorised translation from the second German edition. New York: W Wood [out of print].

Lachs, MS and Pillemer, K (2004) Elder abuse. *Lancet*, 364 (9441), 1263–1272.

Laing, RD (1960) *The Divided Self.* London: Tavistock.

Laming, Lord (2003) *The Victoria Climbié Inquiry.* London: TSO.

Laming, Lord (2009) *The Protection of Children in England: A Progress Report.* London: HMSO.

Langan, J (1999) Assessing risk in mental health, in Parsloe, P (ed) *Assessing Risk in Social Care and Social Work.* London: Jessica Kingsley.

Leiby, J (1984) Charity organization reconsidered. *Social Service Review,* 58 (4), 523–538.

Liegeois, A and Van Audenhove, C (2005) Ethical dilemmas in community mental health care. *Journal of Medical Ethics,* 31, 452–456.

Linehan, MM, Armstrong, HE, Suarez, A et al. (1991) Cognitive–behavioral treatment of chronically parasuicidal borderline patients. *Archives of General Psychiatry,* 48, 1060–1064.

Livingston, G, Leavey, G, Kitchen, G et al. (2001) Mental health of migrant elders – the Islington study. *British Journal of Psychiatry,* 179, 361–366.

LLBC v TG (2007) EWHC 2640 (Fam).

Lolas, F (2006) Ethics in psychiatry: A framework. *World Psychiatry,* 5 (2), 185–187.

Lord Chancellor's Department (1997) *Who Decides? Making Decisions on Behalf of Mentally Incapacitated Adults.* London: HMSO.

Loschen, EL (1974) Psychiatry and religion: A variable history. *Journal of Religion and Health,* 13 (2), 137–141.

Lukes, S (2005) *Power: A Radical View.* Basingstoke: Palgrave Macmillan.

Lupton, D (2000) *Risk.* London: Routledge.

Macdonald, JE and Beck-Dudley, CL (1994) Are deontology and teleology mutually exclusive? *Journal of Business Ethics,* 13 (8), 615–623.

MacPherson, W Sir (1999) *The Stephen Lawrence Inquiry.* London: TSO. Available at: www.archive. official-documents.co.uk/document/cm42/4262/4262.htm

McCubbin, M and Cohen, D (1999) A systemic and value-based approach to the strategic reform of the mental health system. *Health Care Analysis,* 7 (1), 57–77.

McGrath, J, Saha, S, Welham, J et al. (2004) A systematic review of the incidence of schizophrenia: The distribution of rates and the influence of sex, urbanicity, migrant status and methodology. *BMC Medicine,* 28 (2), 13.

McLean, A (1995) Empowerment and the psychiatric/expatient movement in the United States: Contradictions, crisis, and change. *Social Science in Medicine,* 40, 1053–1071.

McMichael, PJ (2004) *Development and Social Change: A Global Perspective,* 3rd edition. Thousand Oaks, CA: Pine Forge Press.

McPherson, B (2008) Equality and diversity as a way of delivering the wider health and social care agenda. *Ethnicity and Inequalities in Health and Social Care,* 1 (2), 4–7.

Masterson, S and Owen, S (2006) Mental health service user's social and individual empowerment: Using theories of power to elucidate far-reaching strategies. *Journal of Mental Health,* 15 (1), 19–34.

Means, R and Smith, R (1994) *Community Care: Policy and Practice.* Basingstoke: Macmillan.

Mental Health Act Commission (2003) *Placed Among Strangers*. MHAC 10th Biannual Report 2001–2003. London: TSO.

Mental Health Act Commission (2005) *In Place of Fear?* MHAC 11th Biannual Report 2003–2005. London: TSO

Mental Health Act Commission (2007) *Risks, Rights, Recovery*. MHAC 12th Biannual Report 2005–2007. London: TSO.

Mental Health Act Commission (2009a) *Coercion and Consent*. MHAC 13th Biannual Report, 2007–2009. London: TSO.

Mental Health Act Commission (2009b) *Women Detained in Hospital*. London: MHAC.

Mental Health Alliance (2002) *Alliance Warns Against Linking Mental Health Reform and Violence*. Press release 30/10/02. Available at: www.mentalhealthalliance.org.uk/news/prviolence02.html

Mental Health Alliance (2003a) *Human Rights in Danger, Alliance and MPs Tell Government*. Press release 11/11/03. Available at: www.mentalhealthalliance.org.uk/news/prhumanrights.html

Mental Health Alliance (2003b) *Draft Mental Health Bill Could Bring Services to Their Knees*. Press Release 19/11/03. Available at: www.mentalhealthalliance.org.uk/news/prservices.html

Merchant, C (2007) Matching skills to need. *Mental Health Today*, April 2007, 23–25.

MIND (2003) *Mind Urges Government to Get Mental Health Act Reform Back on Track*. Press Release 26/11/03. Available at: www.mind.org.uk/news/1986_mind_urges_government_to_get_mental_health_act_reform_back_on_track

MIND (2010) *A Brief History of the User/Survivor Movement*. MIND Information Leaflet. Available at: www.mind.org.uk/help/people_groups_and_communities/user/survivor_empowerment/a_brief_history_of_the_user/survivor_mo

Moncrieff, J (2003) The politics of a new Mental Health Act. *British Journal of Psychiatry*, 183, 8–9.

Morgan, C, Burns, T, Fitzpatrick, R et al. (2007) Social exclusion and mental health: Conceptual and methodological review. *British Journal of Psychiatry*, 191, 477–483.

Morgan, S (2000) *Clinical Risk Management: A Clinical Tool and Practitioner Manual*. London: Sainsbury Centre for Mental Health.

Morgan, S (2004) *Positive Risk-Taking: An Idea Whose Time Has Come*. Health Care Risk Report, October 2004: 18–19.

Morgan, S (2007a) Working with Risk. *Mental Health Today*, 36–37.

Morgan, S (2007b) *Working with Risk Practitioner's Manual. Practice-Based Evidence – A Practice Development Consultancy For Mental Health*. Brighton: Pavilion Publishing.

Munro, K, Ross, MK and Reid, M (2006) User Involvement in Mental Health: Time to face up to the challenges of meaningful involvement. *International Journal of Mental Health Promotion*, 8 (2), 37–44.

Nahem, J (1982) A Marxist approach to psychology and psychiatry. *International Journal of Health Services: Planning, Administration, Evaluation*, 12 (1), 151–162.

National Collaboration Centre for Mental Health (2009) *Borderline Personality Disorder: The NICE guidelines for Treatment and Management, National Clinical Practice Guidance No: 78*. London: British Psychological Society and Royal College of Psychiatry.

National Collaboration Centre for Mental Health (2010) *Anti-social Personality Disorder: The NICE guidelines for Treatment and Management, National Clinical Practice Guidance No: 77*. London: British Psychological Society and Royal College of Psychiatry.

National Confidential Inquiry into Suicide and Homicide (2006) Unpublished sub-analysis from the National Confidential Inquiry into Suicide and Homicide by People with Mental Illness, www.manchester.ac.uk/nci cited in NPSA (2009) *Preventing Harm to Children From Parents with Mental Health Needs*. NPSA/2009/RRR003. Available at: www.nrls.npsa.nhs.uk/alerts/?entryid45=59898

National Institute for Clinical Excellence (2003) *The Clinical Effectiveness and Cost Effectiveness of Electroconvulsive Therapy (ECT) for Depressive Illness, Schizophrenia, Catatonia and Mania. Technological Appraisal TA59*. London: NICE.

National Institute for Mental Health England (NIMHE) (2005) *NIMHE Guiding Statement on Recovery*. London: NIMHE.

National Patient Safety Agency (2009) *Preventing Harm to Children from Parents with Mental Health Needs*. NPSA/2009/RRR003. Available at: www.nrls.npsa.nhs.uk/alerts/?entryid45=59898

National Social Inclusion Programme (2009) *Vision and Progress: Social Inclusion and Mental Health*. London: NSIP. Available at: www.socialinclusion.org.uk/publications/NSIP_Vision_and_Progress.pdf

Neff, JA and Husaini, BA (1985) Lay images of mental illness: Social knowledge and tolerance of the mentally ill. *Journal of Community Psychology*, 13 (1) , 3–12.

NHS Confederation (2010) *Briefing: Delivering Same-Sex Accommodation in Mental Health and Learning Disability Services*. Issue 195. Available at: www.nhsconfed.org/Publications/Documents/briefing_195_same_sex_acc250110.pdf

NHS Modernisation Agency (2001) *The Essence of Care: Patient-Focused Benchmarking for Health Care Practitioners – Benchmarks for Privacy and Dignity*. London: TSO.

Nicholson, J, Sweeney, EM and Geller, JL (1998) Focus on women: Mothers with mental illness: 1. The competing demands of parenting and living with mental illness. *Psychiatric Services*, 49, 635–642.

Nicholson, J, Biebel, K, Hinden, B et al. (2001) *Critical Issues for Parents with Mental Illness and their Families*. Centre for Mental Health Services Research, University of Massachusetts. Available at: www.parentingwell.info.

Nordgren, S and Fridlund, B (2001) Patients' perceptions of self-determination as expressed in the context of care. *Journal of Advanced Nursing*, 35 (1), 117–125.

Nordt, C, Rossler, W and Lauber, C (2006) Attitudes of mental health professionals toward people with schizophrenia and major depression. *Schizophrenia Bulletin*, 32 (4), 709–714.

NSPCC (2009a) *What is Child Abuse?* Available at: www.nspcc.org.uk

NSPCC (2009b) *Signs of Abuse: Learn How to Recognise the Signs of Child Abuse*. Available at: www.nspcc.org.uk

Ofsted (2008) *Learning Lessons, Taking Action: Ofsted's Evaluations of Serious Case Reviews 1 April 2007 to 31 March 2008.* London: Ofsted. Available at: www.ofsted.gov.uk

Olden, M (2003) Obituary: Pete Shaughnessey. *Guardian*, 23/1/07, 22.

Opinion Leader (2009a) *Department of Health Dignity in Care Campaign Case Studies.* Available at: www.dhcarenetworks.org.uk/_library/Resources/Dignity/Dignity_Champion_Case_Studies.pdf

Opinion Leader (2009b) *The Final Report on the Review of the Department of Health Dignity in Care Campaign.* Available at: www.dhcarenetworks.org.uk/_library/Opinion_Leader_Final_Report_to_DH.doc.pdf

Oxford English Dictionary (2009) Pocket edition. Oxford: Oxford University Press.

Oyserman, D, Mowbray, CT, Meares, PA and Firminger, KB (2000) Parenting among mothers with a serious mental illness. *American Journal of Orthopsychiatry*, 70 (3), 296–315.

Parrott, L (2006) *Values and Ethics in Social Work Practice.* Exeter: Learning Matters.

Payne, M (2006) *What is Professional Social Work?* 2nd edition. Bristol: Polity Press.

Percy, Lord (1957) *Royal Commission on the Law Relating to Mental Illness and Mental Deficiency.* London: TSO.

Pereria, S and Dalton, D (2006) Integration and specialism: Complementary not contradictory. *Journal of Psychiatric Intensive Care*, 2 (1), 1–5.

Pernice, R and Brook, J (1994) Relationship of migrant status (refugee or immigrant) to mental health. *International Journal of Social Psychiatry*, 40 (3), 177–188.

Petch, E (2001) Risk management in UK mental health services, an overvalued idea? *Psychiatric Bulletin*, 25, 203–205

Petrides, G, Fink, M, Husain, M et al. (2001) ECT remission rates in psychotic versus non-psychotic depressed patients: A report from CORE. *Journal of ECT*, 17 (4), 244–253.

Philips, P and Labrow, J (2009) *Understanding Dual Diagnosis.* London: MIND.

Pilgrim, D and Waldron, J (1998) User involvement in mental health service development. *Journal of Mental Health*, 7 (1), 95–104.

Pinfold, V, Byrne, P and Toulmin, H (2005) Challenging stigma and discrimination in communities: A focus group study identifying UK mental health service users' main campaign priorities. *International Journal of Social Psychology*, 51 (2), 128–138.

Porter, R (2003) *Madness: A Brief History.* Oxford: Oxford University Press.

Porter, R and Michale, MS (1994) Reflections on psychiatry and its history, in Porter, R and Michale, MS (eds) *Discovering the History of Psychiatry.* Oxford: Oxford University Press.

Pritchard, J (2007) *Working with Adult Abuse: A Training Manual for People Working with Vulnerable Adults.* London: Jessica Kingsley.

Pulzer, M (2008) Negative media coverage of mental health overestimates public dangers. *Mental Health Nursing*, 28 (1), 6.

R v Bournewood Community and Mental Health NHS Trust, ex parte L [1998] 2WLR 764, per. Lord Woolf MR.

R (N) v MHRT (2007) EWHC 1524 (Admin).

R (on the application of A and B) v East Sussex County Council 2003, EWHC 167 (Admin).

R (P) v MHRT East Midlands and North East Region (2002) EWCA Civ 697.

R (Wheldon) v Rampton Hospital Authority (2001) EWHC Admin 134.

Rappaport, J (1984) Studies in empowerment: Introduction to the issue. *Prevention in Human Services*, 3, 1–7.

Rappaport, J (1990) Research methods and the empowerment agenda, in Tolan, P, Keys, C, Chertak, F and Jason, L (eds) *Researching Community Psychology*. Washington, DC: American Psychological Association.

Ray, M, Pugh, R, Roberts, D and Beech, B (2008) *Mental Health and Social Work*. SCIE Research Briefing 26. London: SCIE.

Reamer, FG (2006) *Social Work Values and Ethics*, 2nd edition. New York: Columbia University Press.

Reich, JH and Green, AI (1991) Effect of personality disorders on outcome of treatment. *Journal of Nervous Mental Diseases*, 179, 74–82.

Reich, JH and Vasile, RG (1993) Effect of personality disorder on the treatment outcomes of axis 1 conditions: An update. *Journal of Nervous and Mental Diseases*, 181 (8), 475–484.

Rethink and Turning Point (2004) *Dual Diagnosis Toolkit, Substance Misuse and Mental Health: A Practical Guide for Professionals and Practitioners*. London: Rethink and Turning Point.

Ridley, J and Jones, L (2003) Direct what? The untapped potential of direct payments to mental health service users. *Disability and Society*, 18 (5), 643–658.

Riley, SCE (2002) Constructions of equality and discrimination in professional men's talks. *Journal of Social Psychology*, 41 (3), 443–461.

Risser, P (2003) *Barriers to Self-Determination for People Who Have Been Identified as Having Mental Illness in Western Society*. UIC NRTC 2003 National Self-Determination and Psychiatric Disability Conference Papers. Available at: www.cmhsrp.uic.edu/download/sdconfdoc12.pdf

Ritsher, J, Warner, EB, Johnson, JG and Dohrenwend, BP (2001) Inter-generational longitudinal study of social class and depression: A test of social causation and social selection models. *British Journal of Psychiatry*, 178, s84–s90.

Roberts, M (2004) Psychiatric ethics: A critical introduction for mental health nurses. *Journal of Psychiatric and Mental Health Nursing*, 11 (5), 583–588.

Robertson, M and Walter, G (2007) Overview of psychiatric ethics I: Professional ethics and psychiatry. *Australasian Psychiatry*, 15 (3), 201–206.

Roe, D and Davidson, L (2005) Destinations and detours of the user movement. *Journal of Mental Health*, 14 (5), 429–433.

Rogers, A and Pilgrim, D (1991) Pulling down the churches: accounting for the British Mental Health Users' Movement. *Sociology of Health and Illness*, 13 (2), 129–148.

Rogers, ES, Chamberlin, J, Langer Ellison, M and Crean, T (1997) A consumer-constructed scale to measure empowerment among users of mental health services. *Psychiatric Services*, 48 (8), 1042–1047.

Rojeck, C, Peacock, G and Collins, S (1988) *Social Work and Received Ideas*. London: Routledge.

Royal College of Nursing (2003) *Strategic Plan 2003–2008*. London: Royal College of Nursing.

Royal College of Psychiatrists Social Inclusion Scoping Group (2009) *Mental Health and Social Inclusion: Position Statement*. Available at: www.rcpsych.ac.uk/pdf/social%20inclusion%20position%20statement09.pdf

Royal Commission (1926) *Report of the Royal Commission on Lunacy and Mental Disorders* (Cmd. 2700). London: TSO.

Rush, B (2004) Mental health service user involvement in England: lessons from history. *Journal of Psychiatric and Mental Health Nursing*, 11 (3), 313–318.

Ryan, T (1998) Perceived risks associated with mental illness: Beyond homicide and suicide. *Social Science and Medicine*, 46 (2), 287–297.

Sainsbury Centre for Mental Health (2001) *The Capable Practitioner*. London: SCMH.

Santry, L (2007) *Call to Action as Killings Continue to Fail Service Users and Public*. Available at: www.hsj.co.uk/story.aspx?storyCode=93601

Sayce, L (2001) Social inclusion and mental health. *Psychiatric Bulletin*, 25, 121–123.

Sayce, L and Measley, L (1999) Strategies to reduce social exclusion for people with mental health problems. *Psychiatric Bulletin*, 23, 65–67.

Schnieder, J and Bramley, CJ (2008) Towards social inclusion in mental health? *Advances in Psychiatric Treatment*, 14, 131–138.

Schulze, B and Angermeyer, MC (2003) *Subjective experiences of stigma. A focus group study of schizophrenic patients, their relatives and mental health professionals*. Social Science and Medicine, 56 (2), 299–312.

SCIE (2009a) *Think Child, Think Parent, Think Family: A Guide to Parental Mental Health and Child Welfare*. SCIE Guide 30. London: SCIE. Available at: www.scie.org.uk/publications/guides/guide30

SCIE (2009b) *At a Glance 05: Mental Capacity Act 2005*. London: SCIE. Available at: www.scie.org.uk/publications/ataglance/ataglance05.pdf

SCIE/RCP (2007) *A Common Purpose: Recovery in Future Mental Health Services*. London: SCIE/RCP.

Scottish Executive (2006) *Changing Lives: Report of the 21st Century Social Work Review*. Available at: http://www.scotland.gov.uk/Publications/2006/02/02094408/0

Segal, S, Silverman, C and Temkin, T (1995) Measuring empowerment in client-run self-help agencies. *Community Mental Health Journal*, 31, 215–227.

Shaping Our Lives, National Centre for Independent Living and University of Leeds Centre for Disability Studies (2007) *Developing Social Care: Service Users Driving Culture Change*. London: SCIE.

Shaw, I, Middleton, H and Cohen, J (2007) *Understanding Treatment Without Consent: An Analysis of the Work of the Mental Health Act Commission*. Aldershot: Ashgate Publishing.

Shea, TM, Widiger, TA and Klein, MH (1992) Co-morbidity of personality disorders and depression: Implications for treatment. *Journal of Consulting and Clinical Psychology*, 60 (6), 857–868.

Shift (2006) *Mind Over Matter: Improving Media Reporting of Mental Health.* London: Shift.

Shift (2008) *Mind Over Matter 2: Media Survey Summary Report.* London: Shift.

Shorter, E (1997) *A History of Psychiatry.* Chichester: Wiley.

Singh, SP, Greenwood, N, White, S and Churchill, S (2007) Ethnicity and the Mental Health Act 1983. *British Journal of Psychiatry*, 191, 99–105.

Skodol, AE, Grilo, CM, Pagano, ME et al. (2005) Effects of personality disorders on functioning and well-being in major depressive disorder. *Journal of Psychiatric Practice*, 11 (6), 363–368.

So, AY (1990) *Social Change and Development: Modernization, Dependency and World-System Theories.* London: Sage.

Social Exclusion Task Force (2007) *Reaching Out: Think Family. Analysis and Themes from the Families at Risk Review.* London: Cabinet Office.

Social Exclusion Unit (2003) *Mental Health and Social Exclusion.* London: TSO.

Social Work Task Force (2009a) *Facing Up to the Task. The Interim Report of the Social Work Task Force.* London: DH / DCSF.

Social Work Task Force (2009b) *Building a Safe, Confident Future. The Final Report of the Social Work Task Force.* London: DH/DCSF.

Sorofman, B (1986) Research in cultural diversity: Defining diversity. *Western Journal of Nursing Research*, 8 (1), 121–123.

Spandler, H (2004) Friend or foe? Towards a critical assessment of direct payments. *Critical Social Policy*, 24 (2), 187–209.

Stanley, N and Manthorpe, J (2004) *The Age of the Inquiry: Learning and Blaming in Health and Social Care.* London: Routledge.

Steadman, HJ (1972) The psychiatrist as a conservative agent of social control. *Social Problems*, 20 (2), 263–271.

Storck v Germany (ECtHR; (2005) 43 EHRR 96).

Swanson, KM (1993) Nursing as informed caring for the well-being of others. *Image Journal of Nursing Scholarship*, 25 (4), 352–357.

Szasz, T (1961) *The Myth of Mental Illness.* New York: Paladin.

Szmukler, G (2000) Homicide inquiries: What sense do they make? *Psychiatric Bulletin*, 24, 6–10

Szmukler, G and Holloway, F (2000) Reform of the Mental Health Act. *British Journal of Psychiatry*, 177, 196–200.

Tajfel, H and Turner, JC (1986) The social identity theory of inter-group behaviour, in Worchel, S and Austin, LW (eds) *Psychology of Intergroup Relations.* Chicago: Nelson-Hall.

Tew, J (2007) Power relations, social order and mental distress, in Tew, J (ed) *Social Perspectives in*

Mental Health: Developing Social Models to Understand and Work with Mental Distress. London: Jessica Kingsley.

Thompson, N (1993) *Anti-Discriminatory Practice,* 2nd edition. Basingstoke: Palgrave Macmillan.

Thompson, N (2006) *Anti-Discriminatory Practice,* 4th edition. Basingstoke: Palgrave Macmillan.

TOPSS UK (2002) *National Occupational Standards for Social Work.* Leeds: TOPSS.

Treloar, AJC and Lewis, AJ (2008) Professional attitudes towards deliberate self-harm in patients with borderline personality disorder. *Australian and New Zealand Journal of Psychiatry,* 47 (7), 578–584.

Turning Point (2007) *Dual Diagnosis Handbook.* London: Turning Point.

Uphoff, N (2004) Analytical issues in measuring empowerment at community and local levels, in Narayan, D (ed) *Measuring Empowerment: Cross Disciplinary Issues.* Washington DC: World Bank.

Vanfossen, BE, Spitzer, JJ, Jones, DJ (1981) Social class and emotional distress. *American Sociological Review,* 46 (5), 688–697.

Vaughan, P (2007) Government extends dignity campaign to mental health patients. *Guardian,* 15/08/07. Available at: www.guardian.co.uk/society/2007/aug/15/socialcare.uknews

Vize, C (2007) Mental health: No-one wins in homicide blame game. *Health Service Journal,* 27/11/07. Available at: www.hsj.co.uk/mental-health-no-one-wins-in-homicide-blame-game/293218.article

Wahl, OF (1999) Mental health consumers' experience of stigma. *Psychiatric Bulletin,* 25 (3), 467–478.

Wahl, OF and Aroesty-Cohen, E (2009) Attitudes of mental health professionals about mental illness: A review of the recent literature. *Journal of Community Psychology,* 38 (1), 49–62.

Wallcraft, J and Bryant, M (2003) *The Mental Health Service User Movement in England.* Policy paper 2, Sainsbury Centre for Mental Health. Available at: www.scmh.org.uk/pdfs/policy_paper2_service_user_movement.pdf

Weich, S and Lewis, G (1998). Poverty, unemployment, and common mental disorders: Population based cohort study. *British Medical Journal,* 317, 115–119.

Widiger, TA (2008) Personality disorders, in Hunsley, J and Mash, EJ (eds) *A Guide to Assessments that Work.* Oxford: Oxford University Press.

Williams, GC, Frankel, RM, Campbell, TL and Deci, EL (2000) Research on relationship-centred care and healthcare outcomes from the Rochester biopsychosocial program: A self-determination theory integration. *Family, Systems and Health,* 18 (1), 79–90.

Williams, S (1998) Quality and care: Patients' perceptions. *Journal of Nursing Care Quality,* 12 (6), 18–25.

Williamson, T (2007) Capacity to protect – the Mental Capacity Act explained. *Journal of Adult Protection,* 9 (1), 25–31.

Wilson, M (2009) *Delivering Race Equality in Mental Health: A review.* Available at: www.mentalhealthequalities.org.uk/drereview

Winterwerp v Netherlands (1979) 6301/73, A 33 para 39.

Woodbridge, K and Fulford, B (2003) Good practice? Values-based practice in mental health. *Mental Health Practice*, 7 (2), 30–34.

Woogara, J (2001) Human rights and patients' privacy in UK hospitals. *Nursing Ethics*, 8, 234–246.

Woolhead, G, Calnan, M, Dieppe, P and Tadd, W (2004) Dignity in older age – what do older people in the United Kingdom think? *Age and Ageing*, 33, 165–169.

World Health Organization (1990) *International Classification of Diseases*, 10th edition. Geneva: WHO.

Zimmerman, MA (1984) Taking aim on empowerment research: On the distinction between individual and psychological conceptions. *American Journal of Community Psychology*, 18 (1), 169–177.

Index